MONSTERS
OF PENNSYLVANIA

MONSTERS
OF PENNSYLVANIA

Mysterious Creatures in the Keystone State

Patty A. Wilson

STACKPOLE
BOOKS

Published by
STACKPOLE BOOKS
5067 Ritter Road
Mechanicsburg, PA 17055
www.stackpolebooks.com

Printed in the United States of America

10 9 8 7 6 5 4 3 2 1

FIRST EDITION

Cover art by Marc Radle
Cover design by Tessa J. Sweigert

Library of Congress Cataloging-in-Publication Data

Wilson, Patty A.
 Monsters of Pennsylvania : mysterious creatures in the Keystone State / Patty A. Wilson. — 1st ed.
   p. cm.
 Includes bibliographical references.
 ISBN-13: 978-0-8117-3625-1 (pbk.)
 ISBN-10: 0-8117-3625-3 (pbk.)
 1. Monsters—Pennsylvania. 2. Sasquatch—Pennsylvania. I. Title.
 QL89.W745 2010
 001.94409748—dc22
                          2009051533

CONTENTS

INTRODUCTION

Pennsylvania is home to an assortment of odd creatures, and this volume features the best of the bunch. Bigfoot looms large here, trudging the wilds all throughout the state.

We are all familiar with the concept of Bigfoot. It is the gentle giant of the north woods, fodder for a sitcom like *Harry and the Hendersons*. It's elusive, shy, and eats plants, berries, and bugs. It's rarely seen in urban settings and most stories are about distant sightings.

The Bigfoot is intelligent, curious, sometimes aggressive, and certainly terrifying. He has stalked hikers, hunters, and campers and has even appeared in neighborhoods and farmlands. The creature is massive and could do a great deal of damage if it wanted to. It seems capable of bringing down a deer on foot and killing it with ease. It has an omnivorous diet and possibly uses tools. There is at least one account of a Bigfoot attacking and harming a person. The creature shows remarkable restraint most of the time.

There really is not just one type of Bigfoot in Pennsylvania. The two best known are the five-toed giants, traditionally known as Bigfoot, and three-toed creatures often called Skunk Apes, because of the foul odor they emit. There is also a more elusive, smaller, four-toed beast referred to in native lore as the Apple Picker. Then there is even a classification of super-natural Bigfoot; these creatures exhibit strange characteristics, capabilities, and associations.

Stories of all of these Bigfoot types and other humanoid beasts are included in the first three chapters of this book. The remaining chapters cover other cryptids that inhabit the state. Out-of-place big cats have been spotted in various locations. Large reptilian creatures are found in and near bodies of water in the Keystone State; these creatures include the Broad Top Snake and Bessie, Lake Erie's resident monster. Accounts of attacking airborne creatures, such as gigantic Thunderbirds, are prevalent here as well. And wrapping up the band of fearsome beasts in the state are blood-sucking werewolves and canine creatures. Read on, if you dare.

Classic Bigfoot

When folks think about Bigfoot, they imagine the classic creature of film and lore. They picture the eight-foot-tall, shy monster of the 1967 Patterson film and countless descriptions of an apelike beast wandering the wilderness. In this chapter, I have gathered together some of the most interesting, intense, and mysterious examples of the classic hominid. This is the creature that many suspect lives in remote areas in Pennsylvania and throughout the world. But don't think that classic means common. There is nothing common about encountering a Bigfoot, as the tales that follow amply prove.

Face-to-Face with a Whistling Bigfoot

It was a beautiful summer day in 1835 when a young man decided to set out to pick berries. The blaze of the summer sun on his skin was at once hot and soothing as he stood and picked berries in the woods outside of the town of Bridgewater in Susquehanna County. The young man ate handfuls of berries, hot and sweet, as he dabbled in the sunshine. Suddenly, from a thicket nearby, he heard a sound. The boy was instantly alert for danger. Mountain lions, Indians, and many other dangers could be lurking, waiting to cause him harm.

3

While the young man stood frozen, scanning his surroundings for any sign of danger, he heard the sound again. It was a whistle and he spun around to face it. Shocked, he was mere feet away from a small, black, and hairy creature. The beast was about the height of an eight-year-old boy, but its entire body was covered in coarse hair. The beast walked upright on two legs, and the young man had the distinct feeling that whatever this beast was, it was a juvenile.

The young man just stood and stared. The beast stared back. It pursed its lips and gave out a tentative little whistle. The sound of the beast whistling seemed to break the tension. It then suddenly turned and ran off, still whistling. The young man turned away and ran back toward his home. This is the first known sighting of the whistling beast, but it wouldn't be the last one.

Only about two weeks later in neighboring Silver Lake Township, a similar creature was seen. This time a sixteen-year-old boy was sent into the woods near his home to cut firewood. The boy had taken a gun along for protection and was instructed by his father that he should shoot anything that moved that wasn't human or cattle.

As the boy worked, he heard a rustling in the brush and the sound of whistling, and he supposed that it was his little brother coming to fetch him. The figure walked upright. When it came into view, it startled the boy. The figure resembled a seven-year-old boy in size, but it was covered completely with black hair. The small figure was whistling happily until it saw the boy. The two froze in mutual surprise for a few seconds.

The boy slowly stepped toward his gun and grabbed it. He brought it up and wildly fired off a shot. At the same instant, the small beast jumped behind a tree and ran. Oddly, the beast began to whistle again as it ran through the dense brush away from his attacker.

The boy was so traumatized by the event that he ran home and burst into tears every time he tried to explain to his father what had happened. The father most likely would not have believed his son, if it hadn't been for the Bridgewater sighting approximately two weeks earlier and not far distant from where his son encountered the strange beast.

Pennsylvania Bigfoot Society Investigates Dubois

The following events took place in 2004 near Dubois, and the names of the witnesses have been changed at their request.

Rose and her adult son Brad were looking for a home away from the bustle of city life. They found a little house that was perfect, and Rose loved it at first sight. The little farm was off an old county road and down a short dirt lane. It sat back in the woods with trees all around it. Unless a car passed blaring its radio, they felt as though they were alone in the world. Being isolated was not a problem for Rose or Brad; they enjoyed living in the solitude of the woods. They had almost always lived in the country, and so for them the house was a wonderful find.

For the first few weeks that they lived in the house, they were adjusting to the local noises. Old houses do seem to settle, and the woods often carry their own sounds based upon the time of year and the creatures that inhabit the forest. The snorts of deer and the sounds of night birds were common, as was the occasional bay of a coyote in the distance. At night Rose and Brad often sat on the little porch of the house and chatted about the day. It was a quiet time when they both could reflect, and they enjoyed it very much.

As spring progressed into summer, something seemed to change in the woods around the house. Perhaps the first thing that Rose noticed was that her pets were suddenly very different. Rose had taken in a multitude of cats and several dogs. Although the animals were allowed in the house, they hadn't at first chosen to spend much time there. A wooded hunting lot was a heaven for cats, and during the day, they stayed clear of the house and puttered about in the woods. But as darkness fell, Rose began to realize that the animals were acting strangely. Suddenly, the dogs no longer wanted to venture into the yard to do their business. The cats became clingy and tried to run inside every time the door opened. Rose could not explain the change in behavior, at least not at first.

The dogs drew her attention to the second clue that something was wrong with the woods around the house. Late at night, she and Brad began to hear loud crashing sounds, as if a large creature was moving through the woods surrounding the house. The dogs didn't bark like Rose had expected, but they whimpered and tried to hide under the furniture. It was perplexing to Rose, as were the strange crashes and loud thumps that surrounded her home on more than one night. Rose had at first thought that there were bears around her home, but that didn't explain all the sounds that she heard. Brad asked around and found that no one was seeing bears in the area.

One night, Rose called for her cats and most of them came running. There was a yellow tomcat named Pumpkin that did not come, and that was unusual as he was usually the first one who wanted inside at dusk. Throughout the evening Rose watched and waited, but the cat did not return. Before she went to bed, Rose called for the cat again, but the only thing she heard was the sound of heavy feet running past the house in the woods. It frightened her so badly that she locked her doors and gathered her pets around her in the bedroom.

For several more days, Rose and Brad continued to call for Pumpkin. Pumpkin was a cat that never missed a meal, and so Rose began to wonder if he had been caught in a trap. That was when a second cat suddenly disappeared. Only a week later, one of the older dogs was put out at night and never came back. The animals were acting very strangely. They whined and whimpered as dusk settled in and acted terrified of the darkness pressing in on them. Rose and Brad discussed what was happening with the animals, but they had not come to any conclusions yet.

Early each day, Rose awoke and spent a little time alone. She often watched deer browsing in her backyard while she sipped a strong cup of coffee. She was delighted when the does brought spotted fawns to linger in the early hours. Rose came to expect that she'd see certain groups of deer almost every morning. There was a doe with twins who came every day. Rose sat out a salt lick and posted the ground, so that the deer could have their way. Brad built her a corn trough, where she fed the animals so that they'd linger for her enjoyment.

Then one day the doe came with only one fawn. Rose knew that it was the same doe with the twins, but the other twin was gone. Now she began to pay strict attention to the deer. She realized that a young stag was now missing. She watched and counted the deer and noticed that more were disappearing. At last only a few deer came to her yard. Were they going elsewhere now? Had something frightened them off?

Rose and Brad placed an old burn barrel at the end of the garden. They burned paper garbage and food scraps in the barrel, so that the raccoons would stay away. One night there was a ruckus outside. Rose looked out the windows fearfully, but she saw nothing. She did hear what sounded like heavy feet running past her house, and in the morning she was shocked to find that someone or something had literally torn the barrel in half. Whatever the creature was, it had scooped the foodstuffs from the inside and had eaten scraps that had not burned. She didn't know what to make of the entire situation. There was nothing that she could clearly point to, but there was definitely something frightening in the woods.

Cats continued to disappear, and the wildlife seemed to desert the area. At the edge of the property was a small manmade pond that had been stocked with fish, frogs, and clams. It had been a thriving waterlife community in the beginning of summer, but suddenly the pond was nearly empty. Rose and Brad began watching the pond and one day found large muddy footprints near it. The prints belonged to some large bipedal creature and it seemed evident that it was responsible for cleaning out the stock in the pond. The mother and son found piles of clamshells, as if something had feasted on them. The fish were gone and the pond was empty of all wildlife.

Rose thought it was time to look for help. She checked out the prints on the Internet, but knew that they were not bear tracks. She and Brad came across a Web site for the Pennsylvania Bigfoot Society (PBS) and contacted them. Their president, Eric Altman, opened an investigation, and he and a team made a trip to Dubois to interview the mother and son.

Throughout their investigation, the PBS team found the family truthful and honest. They investigated and set up several trail cameras throughout the woods. The cameras did not produce any evidence of Bigfoot activity, but PBS believed that the story Rose and her son told was true. The PBS team scoured the woods looking for evidence of any creature near the house. During their searches, they turned up several dead cats and deer in the woods near the farmhouse. Something had killed the animals, but not with guns, arrows, or knives. The remains seemed to have been wrung to death or pulled apart. The carcasses were badly decomposed because of the summer heat.

One of the strangest features of the case was the bizarre behavior of the pets on the little farm. On several evenings the PBS team watched the behavior of the remaining cats and dogs as dusk fell. The animals seemed terrorized. They whined, whimpered, and clawed to get into the house. Once inside they slunk off to hide under furniture, and the cats occasionally hissed at something that the humans could not hear.

During one of the PBS visits, the investigators heard about a cat that had disappeared days earlier. As the team checked the outbuildings, they heard a faint mewling sound beneath one of the sheds. It took them hours to locate the missing cat. It was absolutely terrified of something and refused to come out, even when food was placed near it. The cat was disheveled and nearly hysterical as one of the team wiggled under the shed to catch it. The cat was not wedged in or trapped. It was choosing to starve to death rather than to come out from under the protection of the shed.

The team spent some time at the little farm documenting the facts of the case. One of the team members who lived in the area became a liaison between the PBS and Rose. He knew that Rose and Brad were still reporting the strange sounds of heavy footfalls around their home at night. Despite the fact that Brad and Rose now kept all the animals in at night, there were still pets that turned up missing. The team member tried to be a source of comfort for the beleaguered family. One day he tried to make contact and found that the phone was disconnected. He drove out to the little farm and was surprised to find that the house was empty. For some reason, Rose and Brad had moved away rather quickly, without letting anyone at PBS know what had happened.

The PBS noted the case and filed it. There was nothing else that they could do. Was it a Bigfoot? PBS is unable to say for sure, but something was terrorizing Rose, Brad, and their pets.

The Montgomery County Gorilla Case

In the early part of the last decade, the Pennsylvania Bigfoot Society and affiliated organizations investigated several unusual cases. The following story came from the case files of the PBS affiliate in Montgomery County. Fictitious names have been given to those involved, because the actual names were withheld in the file.

The Johnson family lived in a nice little town in Montgomery County. There wasn't much to differentiate their home from those of the neighbors, except for one thing: It seemed to draw the interest of a Bigfoot in the first years of the twenty-first century.

It all began one night when Mr. and Mrs. Johnson were getting ready for bed. Their bedroom windows were approximately twelve feet off the ground, and they never worried about someone peeping in. The Johnsons had barely settled into bed when they heard the terrifying sound of hoarse, raspy breathing coming from the one window nearest the bed. It sounded almost as if someone was just outside the window having an asthma attack. The couple held a whispered conference, trying to figure out what was outside their window. Neither dared to get up and look out. Whatever was breathing loudly on the other side of the pane of glass, it had to be very large. The frightened couple lay petrified until sleep overtook them.

The next morning, Mr. Johnson hurried outside. He found two large footprints of bare feet in the flower bed below the window. The footprints were much larger than Mr. Johnson's own slippered feet, and he shuddered as he stared at them. That creature had to be twelve foot tall to leave prints like that, but there was no creature in Pennsylvania that fit that description—at least no known creature.

For several nights nothing further happened. The couple began to think that they could write the experience off as overactive imaginations. Then it happened again. This time is was a soft winter's night with a gentle snow falling. The Johnsons had just settled down for the night when they both froze.

The same rough, asthmatic breathing came from the window by the bed. The curtains were drawn and the couple lay in the dark listening for several minutes to the sounds of breathing and scratching. At last they heard footfalls as if the creature was leaving, and the couple closed their eyes.

The next morning, Mr. Johnson again hurried outside before anyone else was stirring. The snow carpeted the ground, leaving everything evenly coated with a layer of white. Below the window of the bedroom, he found the same large footprints, but this time the tracks moved across the yard to the horse corral. The tracks showed that the creature had paused by the horses. Inside the corral, Mr. Johnson saw the trampled snow where the horses had panicked. They had apparently vaulted over the four-foot-high fence and run.

Mr. Johnson and his neighbors rounded up the horses and penned them back up. He showed a neighbor the strange footprints; neither man could make sense of the tracks. It would have taken a giant to make tracks that large.

Several days later, the Johnsons' teenage daughter caught a glimpse of something moving outside the house. She went to the patio doors to view it more clearly. As the girl watched, she thought at first she was seeing a horse on the hillside, but the dark animal turned and moved toward the house. It was then that she could see that the dark creature was walking upright like a man and was covered in dark fur. The animal stepped into the woods and disappeared. The daughter was upset by her sighting and told her parents immediately. It was after the Johnsons spoke to their daughter that they decided to contact someone about the creature. A bit of research took them to the PBS Web site and they made contact.

After listening to the Johnsons' reports, PBS assembled a team to investigate. The team soon learned that the Johnsons were not the only ones affected by the creature. Their neighbors also reported strange sounds and odd behavior from their pets. The Johnson house, however, seemed to be the center of the activity.

The PBS team found that some of the footprints still remained in the snow, and they followed them as well as the tracks of the horses across the road. Was a Bigfoot following the horses?

During the investigation, the creature was heard several more nights at the same bedroom window. It seemed that something was drawing it to that particular area.

The PBS investigators also noted that the creature seemed drawn to that area by the trail in the snow that led to the same spot repeatedly. One of the investigators for the PBS was a wildlife biologist, and he began to wonder exactly what held the beast's interest. If he could locate the lure, then he could potentially figure out a way to bring the big-footed creature in.

The biologist noticed that the creature seemed to be particularly drawn to the basement window below the bedroom window. He looked into the room and thought he saw something, but he couldn't quite believe his eyes at first.

Sitting on a rocking chair before the window was a large, stuffed gorilla wearing an Hawaiian shirt. Was it possible that the creature spotted what it thought was another of its kind in the house? The wildlife biologist alerted his team to the potential lure. The team moved the stuffed gorilla and the family did not report any further encounters.

The Creature of Muddy Creek

Allen Hillsmeier lived with his family at Muddy Creek, outside of Delta in York County, near the Maryland border, back on an old road in the woods. He did not believe in monsters, certainly not Bigfoot, but on February 2, 1978, he would make a discovery that would change his life.

On that cold winter's morning Hillsmeier and his son, Jeff, carted the garbage down to the dump site on their land. While they were there, Jeff suddenly noticed some strange footprints in the icy snow. He called his father's attention to the footprints, which were like nothing Hillsmeier had ever seen before. The prints belonged to a large, bipedal creature with three big toes and were sixteen inches long and six inches wide.

Hillsmeier and his son decided to follow the tracks for a distance. Eventually, they counted more than two thousand footprints in the ice and snow. The tracks moved through thick brush and trees, crossed the creek, and then disappeared over the side of a hill. Hillsmeier called a halt to the tracking at that point. The two were now quite a distance from home, and Hillsmeier had begun to wonder about what type of creature could make such large prints.

The father and son returned to the house and told the family of their discovery. Hillsmeier's other two sons wanted to go see the tracks, and so Jeff volunteered to show them to his brothers. In the meantime, Mr. Hillsmeier decided to call the Pennsylvania Game Commission.

Hillsmeier would later say, "They just laughed at me. They told me they were probably deer tracks. That's when I decided to call the newspaper, because I wanted somebody to come here and look at these things." Hillsmeier then called the closest newspaper, the *Aegis* of Bel Air, Maryland, about the footprints on the farm.

The reporter who answered the call to the *Aegis* was Don Morrison, the paper's sportswriter. He passed the call on to Mac Lloyd, who decided to brave the bitterly cold day and go take a look at the footprints. Morrison decided to come along, because nothing was happening at the office that cold Saturday afternoon. Morrison and Lloyd met Hillsmeier at his rural home and rode with him down into the woods on a tractor to check out the prints. The boys were already following the prints. What struck the reporters was that there was a five-foot stride between the prints. A stride like that meant this was a large animal that could have walked on its hind legs for miles and miles.

Hillsmeier said that he did not believe in Bigfoot, but that he was certainly in awe of the tracks. The reporters felt the same. If the tracks had been made by a prankster, they were the work of a very serious prankster. He had braved below-zero temperatures to go out in the woods on the Hillsmeier property and somehow contrive to create the large tracks without any trace of a human around. He had left tracks for miles, crossed streams, climbed hills, and walked miles more, all in the hopes that the Hillsmeiers would find the tracks, be intrigued, and call in authorities. It was certainly not a sure bet as far as pranks go.

By now the reporters were becoming even more fascinated by the footprints. They followed Hillsmeier and Jeff, who had joined them at the site, through the woods. They came upon very clear tracks still frozen in the snow and undisturbed. The tracks had to have been made very recently, because there had been a snowfall only a couple days earlier and they would have been buried.

The group followed the tracks into the brush, where they found the remains of a rabbit—some fur, a piece of the leg, and a few drops of blood. They continued on to an old barbed-wire fence. There Lloyd found dark matted hair caught in the fence. The hair was nearly a foot long and didn't appear human. What type of wild animal could leave such a specimen? Hillsmeier agreed that there were plenty of bear, deer, and other wildlife around his home, but he knew of no creature that could leave bipedal footprints with such a stride and deep imprint, with hair that was nearly a foot long.

Lloyd wrote an article about the strange prints that included information given to him by the Hillsmeiers. Hillsmeier's wife related that only a few days before the prints were discovered, the family dogs had been restless and barked throughout the night. They did not usually seem agitated, but they had been lately.

Hillsmeier and the reporters decided to continue pursuing the mystery of the strange tracks. They learned that a local ecology teacher at Bel Air High School, Bob Chance, was also considered an expert on Bigfoot research. They contacted Chance and asked him to meet them at the site in the woods where the prints were found.

Chance had earned a reputation for being a serious and careful Bigfoot researcher throughout the years. He was a naturalist who had become interested in the subject after having his own close encounter with a Bigfoot in the same area. Chance carefully examined the prints and declared, "I'd say that on a scale of 1 to 10 this rates as an 8. It looks as though he has definitely been here. All the signs point in that direction. The way he moves, his habits, and most of all, his footprints and stride match-up very well with other reports we've had."

Chance and the Hillsmeier boys walked along the trail for some time. They found other hair samples and rabbit parts that looked as if they had been eaten raw. The photographs and samples were sent away to be analyzed.

Chance related that six years earlier he had been hiking with a group of teens from his school in an area near the Hillsmeier farm, when he and the young people had seen a large, hairy bipedal creature that had thrown a large rock at them before running away. Chance was excited by this more recent sighting in the same area.

The hair samples were sent for testing and were returned with the label, "from an unknown creature." Chance continues his work with Bigfoot research and Allen Hillsmeier has become a researcher in the field, too. The question of what had been walking through the woods near the Hillsmeier house would never be answered, but there are those in the field of Bigfoot research who think that they might know the answer.

Bigfoot Stalks York County

Allen Hillsmeier's first encounter with the strange creature known as Bigfoot came when he and one of his sons found large footprints on their rural property at Muddy Creek in York County. Hillsmeier had become intrigued by the strange three-toed tracks that he had seen on his farm. He was a physicist and his mind simply wouldn't allow him to dismiss this modern mystery. He joined forces with Mike Asselin, a chemical engineer who worked with him at the Aberdeen Proving Grounds, to look into the mystery. The two men created an organization called Bigfoot Investigations.

Once Hillsmeier and Asselin began their quest for the truth, they would come to learn that the incident at Muddy Creek was not an isolated event. Two weeks before Hillsmeier discovered two thousand tracks on his farm, a man in nearby Fawn Grove reported seeing a large hairy creature walking upright. He estimated that the man-beast was ten feet tall. He also said that it stunk horribly.

A month after Hillsmeier's encounter, a truck driver from Baltimore was traveling down the road that led to the Peach Bottom Atomic Power Station in York County one night when he saw "a whopper of a man" dash across the road. Two guards at the plant reported that they heard "pig-like" squeals that same night. The noises disturbed them so much that they mounted a search, in which they found large three-toed footprints. They did not see the creature that made them, however. Several locals also reported hearing strange shrieks, cries, and screams that were not quite human. In the weeks that followed, another cryptozoologist, Bob Chance, investigated the area.

Meanwhile, other strange events occurred across the border in Maryland. At Madonna Landfill, adjoining York County, three German shepherd dogs were attacked and one was nearly killed. Afterward, the dog would no longer perform its task of protecting the landfill, for it was afraid of the dark and strangers after its traumatic encounter. In Jarrettville, Maryland, a farmer named Holden found twenty-five of his chickens dismembered and drained of blood. Large, three-toed tracks led away from the coop where the chickens had been killed.

Whatever was stalking the woods at the border did not go quietly away. The following December, Bigfoot Investigations received a report from a hunter at the Holtwood Dam. He had heard a large creature crashing through the brush. The beast seemed to be aware of the hunter, because when he stopped to listen, the creature paused too. The hunter heard a crash to his left and saw a seven-foot-tall humanoid creature running rapidly from the direction of some gunshots that had just broken the silence seconds earlier. The hunter insisted that it was not a human being. He felt intimidated, but later returned to the spot and found the now-familiar three-toed footprints that Hillsmeier first saw.

Through the years, Hillsmeier and Asselin collected many stories from York County. Even today the area is considered a hotbed for Bigfoot sightings. The creatures that stalk the area do not seem inclined to leave, and it has been estimated they have been here for hundreds of years. Human habitation might make life more difficult for this reticent creature, but it doesn't seem willing to move on to less populated areas.

Incident at Lutherlyn

For young Eric Altman, church camp each summer was just a part of the fabric of his life. In the early 1980s, he and his family attended the Lutheran church in his hometown, and each summer he went to Camp Lutherlyn near Butler. Although Eric attended for several consecutive years, there would be one summer when something truly strange occurred. The events that year when he was eleven years old have stayed with him until this very day.

It was hot and humid that year at camp, with kids running around in the woods by day and sleeping on the ground at night. There was swimming and hiking, skits and stories, and tons of hot dogs and hamburgers.

Each camp group got a chance to spend one night at the far edge of the church compound in the primitive campsite to sleep underneath the stars. That was what Eric and his friends at Camp Lutherlyn were looking forward to that very evening. At about 3:00 P.M. the children were told to gather their sleeping bags and other gear and meet near the cabins where they stayed. Their counselors, mostly older teens and young adults, prepared for the outing by loading up coolers with hot dogs and bags of marshmallows for the campfire.

The kids marched from their cabins to the very edge of the church property. There was a field of corn growing tall and green, a little meadow, and then more woods. The kids made their way several hundred yards into the woods and waited for the counselors to assign them an area to put down their sleeping bags. Eric and his friends followed the counselors' instructions, and they ended up in a spot where they could clearly see the stars at the edge of the little meadow that night.

As soon as the sleeping bags were dropped, the children went to work. There was a large fire ring that needed firewood. They'd need plenty of good marshmallow and hot dog sticks, too. Counselors supervised every phase of the event as the children brought in scavenged wood and piled up their sticks for suppertime.

The children played, laughed, and had a great time. Then they washed up and ate their evening meal. With their stomachs full, they played some more. Groups of children occasionally followed a counselor into the woods to drag back wood to keep the fire burning. At about 9:00 P.M., the counselors gathered the children together for the evening events. They sang songs, roasted hot dogs and marshmallows, and laughed at skits the counselors performed by the fire. With the darkness came a chill in the air, and eventually the counselors allowed the children to tell ghost stories. At about eleven o'clock, Eric and his friends tumbled into their sleeping bags to laugh and talk and fall asleep. They were very happy. It was how church camp always was. The last thing that Eric remembered was looking up at the stars in the velvety sky and knowing that this was a grand adventure. Beside him slept his best pal, Ernie, who was likewise a veteran of many church camp summers.

Then, something roused Eric from his sleep. There was a weight across his arm and he couldn't move it. He turned to look and saw Ernie leaning over him. "Don't move," he whispered. "Something's in the woods. The counselors are all upset."

Eric turned his head and saw counselors with flashlights hurrying away toward the fire ring, in which there was still a faint glow from the coals. Something or someone quite large in the woods was making a lot of noise and breaking the branches of the trees. Whatever it was sounded large and mad.

Eric sat up inside his sleeping bag and shared a concerned look with Ernie and the other boys in his group. Instinctively, they were all quiet. In the distance they could hear some of the male counselors shouting into the woods. They were telling whomever was out there to stop acting up. They explained that they were a group from the church camp and said that the person had to stop because he was scaring the children. Yes, the children were frightened, but the counselors' voices seemed imprinted with fear, too.

One of the male counselors ran back to a knot of female counselors and had a quick conference with them. The young women began circulating among the children, calming and hushing them. They told the children to gather up their sleeping bags as quietly as possible and follow them. The female counselors moved quickly and efficiently. They gathered the children together and took them into the cornfield where they all hunkered down to await further instructions. The counselors cautioned the children not to make a sound no matter what.

Eric and his friends waited in the cornfield and listened. Their minds tried to make sense out of what they were hearing. Suddenly, the male counselors returned, but now they had their flashlights off. They glanced over their shoulders as if frightened that something was following them. The counselors whispered among themselves for a few seconds, and then the male counselors moved off again and began to shout at the unseen person making all of the noise. The other counselors hushed the children and told them that on their signal they were to move quietly and rapidly out of the area.

As the children sat in the cornfield awaiting the signal to leave, the beast began to move nearer to them. Eric heard it crashing through the saplings and brush in his direction. He heard it step into the cornfield not far from where he sat and he strained to look up. The noisy beast walked past him hidden by the tall green stalks. At that moment the counselors gave the frightened children orders to move, and they hurried to the safety of the cabins.

The next day the children began to talk. Some of them said that they had heard the counselors mention Bigfoot. Others had already made that assumption. For Eric, it was a singular event that he would relate through the years many times.

In the Woods

The following events took place in November 1993, and the names have been changed at the request of the witnesses.

Dan checked his gear to make sure that it was secure and climbed into his pickup truck. He was on his way to his Uncle Matt's home in Clearfield County to go hunting. These trips were a family tradition, and Dan always looked forward to them. He had spent four years in the Marines and was quite adept at roughing it and handling a vast assortment of weapons. The hunting trip was not just a family tradition for Dan, however, it was a way of life.

Dan drove in the cold along roads that he knew well. His uncle had moved to the rustic mountain area many years ago. Most people think of Pennsylvania as "civilized," but that is because they think of cities like Philadelphia and Pittsburgh. There are vast stretches of mountains in the state that are uninhabited, and Clearfield County still offers rough and rugged areas virtually devoid of human habitation.

The drive to his uncle's house took just under six hours, and Dan was glad to pull into the driveway of the big ranch house. He recognized one truck as his father's and a couple other pickups that belonged to some cousins. The first day of buck season was a state holiday for Pennsylvanians. It came on the Monday after Thanksgiving. Dan smiled and hefted his .30-30 rifle out of the truck. Uncle Matt greeted him at the door. "Mother, fetch Dan a beer," he called. "If it isn't our officer of the peace," he said, slapping Dan on the back. "Come on in son, put your stuff in the corner over there and take a load off."

Dan stowed his gear in a corner of the big living room and accepted the beer and a hug from his Aunt Midge. "Are you hungry?" she smiled.

Dan wasn't overly hungry, but it would hurt his aunt's feelings not to be able to feed him, so he agreed to a turkey sandwich and sat down.

It was a pleasant night with a couple beers and stories that Uncle Matt and Dan's dad always told. It was part of the ritual. Dan couldn't imagine missing buck season.

In the darkness of early morning, Dan rolled over and moaned as he felt his dad tap his leg. "Time to get up, son. Aunt Midge has coffee and breakfast waiting." Dan could smell the aroma of a sturdy breakfast of meat, eggs, and toast. They all wolfed it down and followed it with large mugs of bitter coffee. Then they donned their outside clothes, pulled on their boots and gloves, and hefted their packs up. Each man picked up his gun and they headed out to Matt's old Jeep.

"I've been scouting for months," Matt informed the group. "I found an old log trail that takes ya about three miles back in the woods. There have been plenty of deer rubbings and tracks all through the area. We can drive that far and then take off on separate trails from there if you would like."

Everyone agreed to the plan and they piled in. Matt followed the main roads up into the Pennsylvania State Game Lands and then chose one dirt trail after another as he wended his way ever further into the woods. By the time he stopped, it was daylight and the men could see that they were far from civilization.

Matt pulled the Jeep off in a wide spot. "From here, we walk," he informed them and pulled out a map. "I wanted to show you this so you'll have an idea of the lay of the land. There are trails down here . . . and here," he drew his finger across the route. "There's some nice valleys in here and we should find good hunting."

The men piled out of the Jeep and split up. Dan found a little valley with snow-covered hills and a shelter in the trees on the valley floor. He pulled off his pack and sat down. Lunchtime gave way to late afternoon and Dan waited. He'd seen several startled does, but not the buck he was looking for. He would only take a shot if it was a clean one.

Dan moved around a bit to keep his circulation going. It was cold and the wind bit his cheeks, but Dan didn't mind. He was well dressed for the weather and knew what to expect before he had headed into the mountains.

Suddenly, a distant sound caught Dan's attention. In the crisp air the sound was hard to place. It was almost a grunt or cry, but he had never heard anything like it in the woods. For a long time Dan sat still listening to the sounds, trying to make sense of them. He would have sworn he knew every animal's sound, but this one stumped him. He suddenly realized that whatever was making the sound was now moving in his direction.

Dan stood up. The hackles at the back of his neck were up. He hated that feeling. Never before had he felt unprotected or frightened in the woods, but now he was feeling like prey.

The sounds came closer and Dan heard the creature smashing through the underbrush. He watched the hills that surrounded him with a practiced eye. There was definitely something large out there, and he had the distinct impression that the beast knew that he was there and was trying to frighten him.

At this point, Dan was tracking the creature with his ears and it was directly in front of him in the tree line on the hill above him. He didn't see it move, but he could hear the cries and the sound of large branches being broken and smashed. Whatever it was, this creature was big and could do damage.

Dan felt his hand shake in reaction to the being on the hillside. Every sense in his body told him to get out. He reached down and shouldered his backpack. He stepped lightly as he moved through the woods away from the hillside and the beast that was still raging and smashing limbs.

Dan made it back to the vehicle before darkness fell and waited for the others. His nerves were attuned as they had never been since he had returned from combat. He could not have proven it in a court of law, but Dan knew that he had been stalked and that the creature that had stalked him wanted to frighten him away. It had succeeded admirably.

Dan's dad returned to the vehicle, and Dan quizzed him about the sounds that he had heard. His dad also heard them but said that he hadn't paid them much attention since they were in the next valley over and moving away from him. No one else had heard the sounds, but they all could see how seriously Dan was taking the event. He shuddered as he described what had happened.

Dan would take a lot of teasing about running away from a Bigfoot, but he never wavered in his story. He was a man who would have said that he was not frightened of anything in the Pennsylvania wilderness before that day. He would never again go into the woods without wondering if "it" was out there waiting for him and watching.

Mystery

In 1978, the Frew family moved into a rented farmhouse on Route 819 in Bell Township, Westmoreland County. On their property also sat a cabin, a barn, and an abandoned one-room schoolhouse. At the time, Sam Frew, his wife Ruth, and their twelve-year-old son had no clue that they were about to embark upon an odyssey into the cryptozoological world that few others have ever experienced. For the first few months that the Frew family lived in the old farmhouse, they had no unusual experiences, but beginning in 1979, they began to hear strange growls and hisses from the woods near their home. They soon learned that some of their neighbors were also hearing the sounds. The Frews were not frightened by the occasional noises, but they were a bit perplexed by them. They'd hear the sounds coming from the woods for a night or two, and then there would be nothing for weeks or months. The growls, howls, and cries, however, would eventually return again.

Ruth began a journal of the various events. After two years of keeping records, she discovered that her family heard the creature more in the summer months. She thought the reason, however, might be because the house windows were open then and the family could hear the beast's vocalizations better. In her journal, Ruth began to call the noisemaking beast "Mystery."

It was not until the spring of 1981 that Sam began to understand what was in the woods in his neighborhood. It was late that night and the family was watching television when they heard a particularly loud screech from outside. Ruth jumped and cried out. The piercing scream startled them, because the storm windows were still in from winter. Sam ran for his rifle and a flashlight. He was tired of the noisy beast. The family had discussed the possibilities of what was making the noises for months, but now Sam was determined to get to the bottom of it. He pulled on his coat and pushed open the door, instructing Ruth to close it but stay nearby. He said not to open the door unless he yelled for her. Sam scanned the area with his flashlight and stepped into the darkness. The sound was coming from a field far beyond the house. Sam walked resolutely up the hill toward the field. Every sense was attuned for sound. Each time Mystery gave a shrill cry, Sam had to force himself not to jump. The sounds were primal and yet somehow too human.

Now in the field, Sam paused and listened again. The darkness and the cold pressed in on him. Suddenly he heard a sound across the field, and he swerved around to walk toward the sound on a path that ran along the edge of the field. He swung the flashlight in a wide arc, and for just a second his beam illuminated Mystery for the first time.

Sam could barely believe his eyes. A humanoid creature had walked through the beam of his flashlight. The beast was about four feet tall, but it was broad, muscular, and heavily built. The beast was covered with coarse hair and its eyes had shown reddish orange in the flashlight. Frightened, Sam pulled up his rifle, held the flashlight in his left hand along the barrel so he could see the beast, and got off a shot. Mystery was only about fifty yards away from him when the gun went off, but Sam heard no cry of pain. Mystery suddenly vanished. Sam turned and hurried back the way he had come to the safety of his own home.

By the next morning, Sam was anxious to return to the site where he shot at Mystery. He looked for hair or blood, some indication that he had hit the beast, but he found absolutely nothing. Even the soil was too hard to allow footprints. Sam and Ruth now decided that they should call the police.

The police didn't scoff as Sam had expected. Instead they gave him a hotline number for a group that researched strange creature sightings in the area. Sam didn't think what he saw was a Bigfoot; after all, it wasn't eight feet tall like the ones in the stories he had heard.

Dr. Paul Johnson and a team of investigators began research at the Frew house that spring. Even they at first didn't see any relationship between Mystery and traditional Bigfoot sightings.

Then on August 1, 1981, Sam was walking along a path across the road from his home. He suddenly stopped when he felt as though he was being watched. As he stood there, he heard movement in the brush off to his right. He began to walk again, but his ears strained to hear whatever or whoever was walking in the dense brush only yards away. The foliage was too thick for him to see anything, but the sound of foot-falls, the snap of twigs, and the crackle of the brush was unmistakable. He then came to a cleared area and froze as he watched a nearly twelve-foot-tall hairy beast walking into the woods. Badly shaken, Sam returned home.

A couple weeks later, a local boy who had been biking along Route 819 roused the neighborhood when he claimed to have seen a ten-foot-tall hairy creature walking upright through the field near the Frew house. The boy watched as the beast crossed the field and disappeared into the woods. The boy was able to observe the beast long enough to describe it as having a conehead, no neck, and brown-black fur all over its large body.

Through the years, Dr. Johnson and his team would spent literally hundreds of hours at the Frew farm and in the surrounding woods. Dozens of creature sightings came from the area where the Frews lived, but by 1984, Johnson believed he was probably never going to solve the Mystery case. He also realized that folks were experiencing something extraordinary in that area, but he could not say for sure exactly what it was.

As the years went by, life moved on for the Frews. Ruth passed away and Sam decided to move. At that point the formal investigations stopped for a while.

Then in 2006, Johnson was contacted by Eric Altman of the Pennsylvania Bigfoot Society. Altman was inquiring about the sightings of a creature that Johnson had investigated between 1981 and 1984. Johnson told Altman about the Frews and Mystery. He listened as Altman explained that he had been contacted by a woman named Lisa who had reported seeing a large hairy man on Route 819 very recently. Altman wondered if Johnson would like to take the case as he was already familiar with the area and the sightings. Johnson agreed to take the case, and early in December 2006, he sat down to talk to Lisa for the first time.

Lisa's story was simple and direct. She had been traveling down Route 819 in the middle of a bright September day. As she drove down a hill, she saw what she first mistook to be a man running down a farm lane. The figure then darted out onto the road in front of her and she saw it more clearly. It was an unclothed humanlike figure with reddish-brown hair covering its entire body. Lisa estimated that it was approximately six feet tall and moved fast across the road. The creature seemed oblivious of Lisa, her large SUV, and everything going on around it.

Lisa stopped and turned at the intersection a short distance away, but saw nothing in the open field beyond the little embankment. She was puzzled because the creature still should have been visible. It had only been mere seconds since she had seen it pass her car, but it was now gone. Lisa looked for the creature from her car for a little bit and then continued on to the town of Apollo. For some time, Lisa mulled over the sighting. The creature didn't seem like Bigfoot to her and she didn't connect the two at first. It took her a while to report it, and she confessed that she had not noticed any significant facial features or other identifying information.

Johnson was struck by the credibility of the young woman. She seemed genuinely puzzled by what had happened to her. After lunch, he asked Lisa to show him where exactly she saw the creature. Lisa agreed and drove out to the top of a little hill. Johnson got out and looked around, smiling. The old Frew farm was just beyond the hill. Much of the topography was still the same despite the passing of twenty years. Yet there were changes. Some buildings had been pulled down, but the old house remained. Johnson could not help but remember the many hours he had spent there with the Frews.

Johnson began his investigation despite the blustery conditions and walked along the sighting area. He looked at the topography and saw why Lisa was so puzzled by the disappearance of the creature in the two or three seconds it took her to stop at the nearby intersection. All that was around the area were open fields, and they should have taken minutes to cross, not seconds. Johnson took photographs and returned to the car. He thanked Lisa for her time and information and returned home. Perhaps Mystery, or another Mystery, was still in the area. Johnson wrote the following paragraph at the end of his discussion of the Frew case in his privately published book *The Bigfoot Phenomenon in Pennsylvania*:

> The preceding two examples from Allegheny and Westmoreland Counties also provide evidence for another characteristic of the Pennsylvania Bigfoot: there appears to be many more than one species of the creature. In Pittsburgh's north hills, both 3-toed and 4-toed animals were observed. In Bell Township there were variations from a very tall ape-like creature to a much shorter, hairy one not really resembling an ape. I started calling the creature observed by Lisa "Geico Man." Although I never saw this type of creature, it has been reported in the past . . . and in my own mind, I imagined that it resembled the Neanderthal-like actors in the television commercial.

Whitey

Bigfoot researchers are limited in what they can do. They can return to the scene of the sightings, set up cameras in case the creatures return, and look for physical evidence, such as hair, scat, and footprints. In large part, though, they must rely upon eyewitness accounts for their background data. They must keep meticulous records so that they can see patterns forming in certain areas. Bigfoot research groups are also in contact with other paranormal research groups, so that they can share data. The following reports were collected by the Center for

Unexplained Events (CUE) and the Pennsylvania Bigfoot Society (PBS). The two groups work together quite frequently and share members. The leader of CUE is Brian Seech, and he is also an active member of several other organizations, including PBS. It was Seech who opened his files and called my attention to this unusual series of encounters.

When a team from CUE received their first call about a sighting of a white creature, it was actually six years after the event. Seech, his wife Terrie, and their team went to check out the story. It was April 2006, and the call came from the New Castle area of Lawrence County. According to the witness, on July 10, 2000, he had been out fishing in a local stream when he suddenly got the feeling that he was not alone. The man looked up, studied the woods, and saw a five-foot-tall, white-haired ape-creature watching him from the opposite bank. The witness described the creature's head as "cone-shaped" and said he saw it so clearly that he could see the wind blowing through the long, white fur on its body. The man estimated that he and the creature could not have been more than twenty feet apart.

The witness didn't notice any smells, sounds, or other odd characteristics, but he and the creature seemed frozen in a staring contest for nearly five minutes by his estimation. Then the man became so unnerved by what he was seeing that he turned and hurried back the way he had come. He said he looked back to be sure that the beast was not following him and saw it still standing there at the tree line.

CUE began its research by looking into their files for other reports from the same area. They found one incident that took place a few miles from where the white creature had been seen at the stream. This report, September 18, 2004, had actually been given by one of Terrie Seech's friends who lived in the area, along the Beaver-Lawrence county line. The woman said that one evening she had been letting her dog out when she saw a red-eyed, white bipedal animal in the woods along the edge of the tree line watching her. The woman reported that although she was startled by the creature, her dog did not seem interested and simply went about its business. The beast stood just below a tree branch and watched the woman and dog curiously. When the Seeches visited the property to investigate, they found no footprints or hair samples, but they were able to determine an approximate height for the beast. In the 2004 report, the woman said the creature's head had almost touched a certain branch on a particular tree, so the Seeches found the tree and measured from the branch to the ground. The measurement showed the beast to be approximately 6 feet, 10 inches tall. Now the CUE team wondered if the two sightings were of the same creature or of two different ones. It was possible that the beast had grown significantly in four years, but they could not rule out any possibility.

Another report of a sighting in the area was also found in CUE's files. This sighting was dated October 8, 2004, and came from a witness near Brady's Run Park in Beaver County, which is well within the twenty-mile radius they were investigating.

According to the report, a young man was laying in a hammock when he suddenly heard what sounded like an animal crashing in his direction, breaking tree branches and stomping the undergrowth. The young man sat up and saw the creature approximately 125 feet away, running through the woods. The beast paused for a moment, as if getting its bearings, before plunging onward. The young man confided his experience to his family; they convinced him to contact CUE.

When CUE investigated, they found broken branches and trampled brush in the right area. They found branches snapped about eight feet, three inches from the ground, so they knew the animal was very large. They found no prints or any other physical evidence of the event.

All of the material reflected an interesting pattern that suggested that one or more albino creatures were in the woods along the border of the two counties, but none of the accounts were as dramatic as the one that was about to occur.

On January 9, 2006, a little boy in the New Castle area went outside to feed his dog. It was approximately 5:30 P.M., so it was dusk. The little boy was walking across the yard when the dog began barking back toward the tree line where something was disturbing it. The boy scanned the area and froze. There in the woods watching him was a large, white beast that was standing upright like a man. The animal seemed to be playing a game of hopping from behind one tree to the next one before stopping to check on what the little boy was doing. That was enough for the child, and he turned and ran for the house.

Inside, the boy told his mother the fantastic tale and she went to look outside. To her surprise, she also saw the bipedal creature at the edge of the woods. Together, the boy and his mother watched the beast for approximately five minutes before returning inside. The animal had stopped hopping around and had taken up a position behind a tree to watch them.

Within a week of the sighting, the mother found the PBS Web site and posted her experience. The Seeches and veteran researcher Paul Johnson read the sighting and contacted the family. The sighting fit the same pattern they had been investigating in the area.

The team interviewed the boy and his mother and asked if they could post game cameras in the woods. The investigators decided to concentrate on an area around a burn barrel, because the family said that they occasionally found bare footprints in the snow there and the barrel had been disturbed as if someone or something had been digging in it.

The team also learned that during the week between the sighting and the team's arrival, the family dog had disappeared.

They thought that it ran away, but the mother wondered if the disappearance of the dog might have any connection to a family member's disappearing cats just down the road a few hundred yards. The CUE team left the game camera in the woods for a week, but did not get a single interesting photo. They are still building a profile for one or more white Bigfoot-type creatures in the twenty-mile area encompassing New Castle and the area just over the Beaver County line.

Gorilla on the Loose

The month of December 1920 was not a normal one for the Bolig family, who lived on a small farm near Meiser, Snyder County. For more than three weeks, the family had been on edge because there had been some strange things going on near their home. Charles Bolig's fifteen-year-old twins, Margaret and Samuel, claimed to have seen a "huge ape" in the woods, and night after night, the family was terrorized by loud screams outside. The local gossip was that a gorilla had escaped from a wrecked carnival train in Williamsport early in the summer, and the animal was believed to be wandering the woods.

The second sighting was more serious. Samuel saw the creature in a field one night and followed it with a light and a gun. He shot at it in the cornfield near the house. According to his testimony later, he shot the beast point-blank in the chest. He thought the beast had been struck, because it fell and rolled away. Seconds later, however, it rose again and ran off. The boy found blood in the field the next morning, but he was unable to track the creature.

As strange as that was, the family was still not prepared for what happened on the evening of December 10. Charles was out chopping wood between seven and eight o'clock in the evening when the children, who were in the house, heard a roaring sound that terrified them. Samuel grabbed his father's .32-caliber revolver and ran outside. Margaret followed her brother out the door.

The children saw a large humanoid animal about ten feet from the house standing under a tree and watching them. Samuel pulled up the gun, but the creature attacked him before he could shoot. Margaret cried out for help and tried to rescue her brother. Charles heard the commotion and came to the aid of the children. The beast ran off when it saw him.

By the time Charles arrived, Samuel was badly injured. The animal had grabbed his leg and torn at his knee, dislocating it by brute strength. It tried to strangle Samuel, knocking him unconscious. Samuel's arm was also twisted and broken. He ended up in bed for days.

The day after the attack, the local newspaper stated that upwards of a hundred armed men were in the woods looking for the beast. Fear ran rampant in the area and many folks walked around armed with guns. For several months thereafter, Snyder and Northumberland counties were rife with sightings of the creature. Samuel later described the attack to a newspaper interviewer. He said on its hind legs, the creature appeared to be seven feet tall. Others who reported seeing the beast described it as brown or black with human features and thick lips. It was usually seen walking on two feet, but some reported that it dropped to all four feet when fleeing.

At the time that the Bolig family first began to hear the creature around their home, they also noticed that someone or something was entering their cellar and stealing food. The family later found footprints from the beast around the cellar door, and they believed that the animal was drawn to the place looking for edible goods. It was December and there was very little vegetation that the beast could eat. The animal seemed particularly partial to the apple bin and left many half-eaten apples behind. The Boligs were not the only ones, however, to find food missing from their root cellars and smokehouses. Fruits, vegetables, and even hams were stolen by the intruder who left behind large prints.

At last the hysteria in the area grew to the point that a reward was offered, supposedly by the carnival company. If the beast was captured alive it was worth $1,000, and if it was dead, $500. Hunters came pouring into the area and bragged that it would only be a matter of days until the beast would be captured, dead or alive. The professional hunters were waiting for the first snow so that they could better track the beast, but the story in Meiser ends there.

Through the following year, however, other similar creatures suddenly began appearing in various areas throughout central Pennsylvania. On December 20, a man named Yeager said a seven-foot-tall beast jumped out in front of his car when he and his family were driving near Lewistown. The creature seemed to attack the car, but missed. Yeager was carrying a gun and he stopped and shot at the monster twice while it was running back into the woods. Then in January, a farmer in Wallaceton, Clearfield County, reported seeing a large hairy beast that walked on two feet attack and kill a calf in the barnyard of his farm. The farmer had discovered the creature eating the calf. This event also set off a major hunt. On February 1, 1921, a similar beast was sighted. This time it was near Pen Mar in Franklin County, according to an article that appeared in the *Gettysburg Times*. The witness was John Simmons, who was walking through a field on his way home that Saturday afternoon. He got a good, clear look at the creature as it ran away from him. From February until August 13, the rash of encounters subsided, but on that day a creature was sighted near York Street in Gettysburg, running off in the direction of Biglerville. On August 20, the beast returned to Gettysburg and once more was seen. This time a load of buckshot was flung in its direction. Later that same night, another creature was reported near Fort Loudon by Howard C. Mitinger of Gettysburg. Mitinger was a public official and had his sister-in-law, niece, and two friends in the car when they all saw the creature. The group insisted that it was a bright moonlit night and they could clearly see it walking along the road.

The last known sighting was on August 27, 1921, when Ray Weikert watched the creature walk across the road in front of his horse. Weikert was riding on Fairfield Road and had to struggle with his terrified horse to keep it under control. He later stated that the beast walked on its back legs like a man and climbed over a fence before disappearing. He described it as approximately five feet tall.

This series of newspaper accounts from the early 1920s leaves more questions than it answers. The behavior and diet of the various beasts reported are clearly not those of a gorilla. Cryptozoologists would see these as classic Bigfoot encounters, but the mystery of the numerous sightings continues to puzzle them to this day.

Incident at East Pennsboro

In the fall of 1985, the area of East Pennsboro Township in Cumberland County became ground zero for a cryptozoological mystery that has yet to be solved.

It all began on September 6 when Edward Kreamer and his girlfriend witnessed a strange sight. They saw a creature approximately six-and-a-half feet tall and covered with fur. The beast seemed to have a head that sat on its shoulders and gave it the appearance of having no neck. The beast had abnormally long arms and gave the general appearance of an ape, except that it walked like a man.

At the time, Kreamer thought that he was seeing a prowler and gave out a loud shout. The figure gave no sign of hearing the shouts and kept going. It was then that Kreamer and his girlfriend observed that this was no ordinary prowler.

Kreamer's cousin was also on the rural property and he was shocked when the beast walked within eight feet of him, near an area where the property owners had dumped some chicken entrails after butchering. Kreamer's cousin said that the beast had big teeth and large claws. Everyone talked about a terrible rotting smell that seemed to come from the beast.

In the following days, a similar creature was seen throughout the area. It was spotted at the local waterworks, approximately five miles away. Others came forward to say that there was more than one such beast.

Kreamer again encountered similar beasts, but this time he saw a large female and a smaller creature that he believed was a juvenile. This time the beasts walked across the road in front of his car. Kreamer's described the larger to be about seven feet tall and covered with charcoal-colored fur.

On another occasion, Kreamer saw what appeared at first to be a prowler on his girlfriend's family property. He ran to the porch after the prowler and then paused when he saw it was another of the creatures. When it stepped in front of a white fence about fifty yards from the house, he saw it quite clearly. It had a long stride and wide, slouching shoulders.

Kreamer, however, was not the only one encountering these creatures. A couple from Michigan visiting the area reported seeing a beast cross the highway in front of their car. On September 26, two men reported smelling a foul odor and saw a "fanged creature" with a fur-covered body and no neck.

When local newspaper reporters interviewed the police chief, he insisted that the entire thing was nothing but a prank. He said that the creature or creatures were teens in costumes. An unnamed witness, however, told reporters, "the creature moved too fast and too fluidly to have been a person in a costume. It had shoulders about three feet wide and stood 6 to 7 feet tall. The head came to a point and was on the shoulders."

Things got more murky on October 11, 1985, when a prankster was arrested after being caught with a fur costume and fanged mask. The prankster said that the sightings had spurred him to create his own costume. He stood at the roadside at night and allowed the headlights to hit him before taking off. He knew nothing, however, about the original sightings and claimed that they were real. He also said that he had nothing to do with the sounds and smells associated with the events.

Heart Attack

The trailer park sat in a rural section of Allegheny County. It was tucked away from the world on three sides by trees. The folks who lived there were mostly friendly, neat people, and so the little trailers were well cared for and had pleasant porches. Among the residents was an old couple who asked to remain anonymous in this account. The couple had a trailer near the end of the lot and not far from the woods. The lot was one of the least expensive, because the garbage Dumpsters were located nearby. Still, it was a quiet spot and the older couple liked it.

One summer in the late 1970s, something changed. Strange sounds began emanating from the Dumpsters late at night. At first the old couple thought that the sounds must have been raccoons digging in the trash bins, but they wondered how the animals were getting the heavy lids up. Then they were even more puzzled when they began to find mounds of garbage piled outside the Dumpsters some mornings. That was when the couple began to think a hobo was living in the woods nearby and that he might be responsible for the garbage mess. Either way, something had to be done, because they couldn't keep picking up the garbage.

The old man began to watch the site carefully. He kept his powerful flashlight with him and sat up late at night waiting for the culprit. That was when he began to smell a terrible stench, like a skunk and a wet dog combined. It was almost overpowering, but it didn't always come from the Dumpsters. It just wafted along from the woods.

Then the old couple began hearing bone-chilling screams. They only heard them a few times, but these were enough to frighten the old couple back into the trailer. The couple determined that they wouldn't put food waste into the trash until pickup day to minimize the scent that was bringing whomever or whatever from the woods.

One night the couple decided to sit up very late and enjoy a cool breeze, because their trailer had been especially stuffy that afternoon. As they sat watching the stars, they heard a slam from the trash area. The old man picked up his flashlight and arose. He walked to the edge of the porch and called out, "Who's there?"

He clicked on the light and moved it around. Suddenly, he saw something in the beam that he could not quite fathom. It looked like a seven-foot-tall man covered in white fur. The beast turned at that moment and bellowed as its red eyes reacted to the strong light. It was standing inside a Dumpster, and it placed one hand on the outer rim of the receptacle and vaulted over the side. With a soft spring, it hit the ground. The old woman screamed and the couple quickly headed indoors.

After calming down, the couple discussed what they had seen. The old woman wanted to call the police, but her husband felt that they would be treated like old fools and decided against it. They described the beast to each other and agreed on what they had witnessed. From then on, the couple only approached the Dumpster in daytime. They now kept their food scraps in a tight-fitting can that sat on their porch, and they disposed of the contents later. They were not aware that other neighbors had been seeing, hearing, and smelling the beast, too. No one wanted to call the police. It just wasn't the sort of thing that sane people should be reporting, they felt.

Everything changed one night in late August when the old couple was sitting up with their front door open, enjoying the cool night air. They were in the dark talking when they heard a terrible crash on the porch. It sounded as if a chair had been smashed. Out of instinct, the old man went to the closed screen door and looked out. Suddenly, he was face-to-face with the albino Bigfoot that was holding the large can that they now used for their food scraps. The old man staggered back and slammed the door. He couldn't talk and his wife realized immediately that there was something drastically wrong. She saw her husband clutching at his chest and ran for the phone. She needed paramedics immediately.

Within minutes, paramedics and police arrived. The old woman told the whole story to the officers. She could tell immediately that they did not believe her. Finally, the older officer told the younger one to take a light and go look around out at the dump in case a vagrant might be lurking there.

Within moments, everyone on the scene heard the young officer scream. The older officer unsnapped his gun, grabbed his powerful flashlight, and took off running. The old woman left for the hospital before they returned, but she and her husband later learned that the first officer saw the white Bigfoot flipping open the heavy lid on a Dumpster and climbing inside. That was when he screamed. The cry had caught the attention of the hungry Bigfoot and it had turned. It was then that the young officer saw that the beast had red, glowing eyes and that it was eating something. By the time the older officer arrived, the beast was vaulting from the Dumpster with a handful of garbage and was running for the woods.

Later, the police contacted a Bigfoot research society in the area and a team was dispatched. The team found large footprints consistent with known Bigfoot prints, but they didn't find the creature. Apparently the beast decided to move on to less conspicuous digs, for it was not seen in the trailer park again.

Encounters on Chestnut Ridge

The Chestnut Ridge, running from Preston, West Virginia, to Indiana County, Pennsylvania, is famous in cryptozoological circles for the many Bigfoot sightings and encounters that have occurred there. Large parts of the Chestnut Ridge are still very rural. For one father and son living along the ridge in western Pennsylvania, their home in the wilderness became a frightening place. In March 2007, the son was unloading his car around 11:30 P.M. one dark night. Suddenly, he heard an unusual, high-pitched chattering coming from the woods about seventy-five yards from the house. He froze at first, as the chatter sent shivers up his spine. Then he broke and ran for the house, as the whistles and screams of what seemed to be some large primate in the woods rang out.

Inside the house, the young man confided what he had heard to his father. After a bit of a pause, his father confessed that he had heard the same sounds a few nights earlier. Neither man could imagine what was causing the sounds, but they were certain that those were not natural sounds in the area.

The man and his son began to suspect that they might have a Bigfoot in the wilderness near their home, and they called in a research team. The team did not find any physical evidence, but a few weeks later UFO and Bigfoot research legend, Stan Gordon, received a report that might have had a bearing on the case.

A hiker had contacted Gordon after finding a series of large, humanistic footprints on the trail he was following. The prints were twice the size of the hiker's foot and the width of the stride between the prints was amazingly large. It was certain that no ordinary man made those tracks.

On April 22, 2007, a young soldier had a strange encounter. He had done a tour in Iraq and was suffering from post-traumatic stress disorder. The nights were long for him, so he began to fish all night long. It was a way to ease his spirit in the tranquility of the waters of the Loyalhanna Creek with the breeze blowing, the moon shining, and the sounds of night echoing. There was one place along the creek, not far from his home, where he particularly liked to fish.

It was about 3:30 A.M. when he noticed what looked like another man in the distance. It seemed a bit odd that another fisherman was out that late at night, so the veteran began to watch him. The figure was splashing in the water and that was unusual. The veteran moved closer with his flashlight to get a better look at the other fisherman, whose back was turned away from him. As the veteran got close enough to make out details, the figure turned toward him. It was a large, hairy creature between seven and eight feet tall. The figure raised a hair-covered arm to shield its eyes from the bright light and stood up. Its hair was wet and matted. It returned a stare before it walked away from him. The young man stood in stupefied silence watching the creature retreat. The veteran's amazement made him step forward and follow the figure toward the banks of the creek.

The veteran kept his tale to himself for a couple weeks, but then he encountered another fisherman on the Loyalhanna, near the spillway one day. The men got to talking, and the other fisherman told the veteran a story that didn't surprise him at all. The fisherman said that one day he had been in the area when he saw a large creature come out of the woods on the far side of the creek. It hunkered down and cupped its hand to get a drink. The fisherman watched the creature in amazement. Suddenly the beast stood up as if sensing that it was being watched and saw the man standing there. It turned and ran back into the woods.

Late in May 2007, at dusk, several teenage boys were riding bikes along a trail that runs along the Loyalhanna Creek. They were about five miles away from the spillway when they heard the sounds of something large moving along the other side of the creek. As they tried to make out what it was, they suddenly saw a large, hairy creature moving on two feet along the creek. The beast was walking from tree to tree, watching the boys. It leaned forward to peek around the tree and then pulled back.

Little did the boys know that this is a behavior that is well documented in Bigfoot sightings. The creatures exhibit intelligence and curiosity about the humans they encounter. The boys watched for several minutes before they broke and turned back toward town, riding as fast as they could away from the beast. Occasionally, they'd pause to see if the beast was following them, and to their horror, it was. They caught it darting between trees and peeking out when they paused. It never tried to cross the creek to get closer to them, but it was curious about them. The young boys and their families have ignored attempts by the investigators to contact them, however.

These are only three of the dozens of reports that have come from the Chestnut Ridge area each year.

The Jacobs Photos

In 2007, the Bigfoot community was rocked by what would become known as the Jacobs photos. The Jacobs family attached a camera to a tree in the woods near their home to get shots of deer and other wildlife in the Allegheny National Forest. What they captured in the photos was a large, black-furred creature that was slim and appeared to use two feet. The beast was believed to have been a juvenile Bigfoot. The Pennsylvania Game Commission quickly offered its own estimation that it was a bear with a bad case of mange. For one anonymous park ranger, however, the photos were shocking. He recognized the creature as something else.

Previously, in October 2007, this ranger was patrolling the park by vehicle when he turned onto a forest maintenance road. It was not a well-traveled trail, and he had no expectations other than that he might see a bear or a deer along the path. As the ranger entered a cleared area, he saw an embankment across a field, where a large, black creature was leaning forward eating berries. The creature's back was to the ranger as he pulled to a stop.

The ranger had a camera with him and he decided to get a photograph of what he assumed was a large black bear eating berries. He slipped out of his vehicle and ran across the field, camera in hand. He watched as the animal turned and shuffled down the embankment on its back legs. This was odd behavior for bears, which usually walk on all fours. The beast had slid down the far side of the embankment, so the ranger thought that it was safe to go to the top of it and snap photos of the bear in retreat. He climbed the embankment and watched the beast.

Whatever the creature was, it dropped to all four feet and began to shuffle off. The beast ran into a thicket of briars and disappeared. The ranger had gotten a good look at the creature, and he was surprised to note that the beast had red-tipped black hairs. Black bears usually do not have a red tip or tinge to their fur.

Another thing that the ranger noticed was that the back end of the animal was raised up higher than the front end. Bears do not have longer legs in the back than in the front. This creature did have longer back legs, giving it a tilted profile.

The ranger was puzzled by the creature. It was not a bear in his estimation. It was not what he had heard Bigfoot should look like either. He was not really sure what to make of the beast. It was not like any known large animal in Pennsylvania's wilderness. The ranger was so puzzled that he contacted the Pennsylvania Bigfoot Society and made a report. He did not think that it was a Bigfoot creature, but he thought that some formal report should be made of the beast.

When the Jacobs photos were released months later, the ranger immediately recognized the creature as similar to what he had seen. He recognized the longer back legs, the strangely humanoid body, and the odd stance. The creature in the photos has never been identified conclusively.

Sam Sherry's Encounter

In the realm of Pennsylvania's Bigfoot research, there are certain names that are famous, among them Sam Sherry and Dr. Paul Johnson. Sherry came to the notice of the world in 1988. Johnson, a professor at Duquesne University in Pittsburgh, has been heavily involved in Bigfoot and UFO research for many years. Sam called Johnson in December 1988 to say that he encountered a Bigfoot in Westmoreland County seven months earlier, in May. He said that he'd be willing to talk about his strange sighting, but Johnson had to visit him at his home.

When Johnson arrived, he met a nice older couple. Sam's wife, Naomi, served up coffee and old-fashioned hospitality. Sam, a rather old man who was still a hearty outdoorsman with a rough, leathery face, waited for his guest to get comfortable before he began.

"I was told that you and some other folks are collecting material on those Bigfoot things folks are seeing out this way," he said. Johnson agreed that was true. Then he heard one of the most amazing tales of a Bigfoot encounter that he had collected to date.

According to Sam Sherry, his encounter began when he pulled into a favorite fishing spot along the Loyalhanna Creek, not far from Ligonier on Route 30. It was 11:30 P.M. when Sam pulled his blue 1975 Maverick near the creek. In the back of the car were all of the fishing supplies that Sam needed. It was

May 17, and it was a cool, clear night with a bright moon shining across the water and lighting the woods. Sam had fished that spot many times and he was looking forward to the night.

While Sam was unloading his gear, he began to notice a strange smell. It was a musty smell that he would later describe as "foul damp air." It reminded him of a damp, musty cellar or a wet dog.

Suddenly, a strange sound from across the road broke the pleasant silence of the night. It was as if there were gorillas in the woods. A monkey-like chattering sound was followed by guttural grunts, whistles, and squeals. It was the strangest thing Sam had ever heard coming from the woods. Along with this were the sounds of walking, brush crashing, and branch snapping. Sam looked up sharply toward the sounds and was shocked to see glowing orange eyes moving in his direction. The eyes were reflective, but much too high and large for a deer or even a bear. He saw nothing but the eyes coming his way.

Then, at the edge of the woods, maybe twenty feet from Sam, a figure materialized. Sam's first observation was that it "appeared," not moved into the area, for he had neither seen nor heard it move to that spot. It simply appeared there with its glowing eyes watching him.

Sam stared at the strange creature in wonder. It was like nothing he'd ever seen before. The skin on the beast was leathery, brown, and wrinkled. It was as if the creature was old and worn. He got the impression that it was as if it had mange. Although the beast was similar to a human, it didn't have the curves of a human body. It was bigger than a human, and it had arms much longer than human arms. The head sat squat on the shoulders, giving it the appearance of almost having no neck. The orange eyes were huge. The face was also leathery and gave the appearance of great age. The creature had two ears tucked close to its head and there was a wide strip of hair down the middle of its head, like a Mohawk haircut. The sides of the head along the Mohawk were bare, but there were two patches of hair around each ear.

The beast watched Sam studying it. Its breath wheezed loudly as spittle shot out of its mouth. It seemed to have difficulty breathing and swallowing. It then let out a mighty sigh.

Suddenly, the beast broke off eye contact and began to posture and grunt as if challenging Sam's right to be there. It flexed, bellowed, and thumped its chest.

Sam now realized how vulnerable he was. He got the impression that the beast was putting on a show for other animals. Sam's eyes squinted to look for them, but he saw none. He was sure, though, that other creatures were watching in the darkness. Curiosity now won out over fear, and Sam continued to watch. His woodsman's instincts told him that this creature was only posturing and was not dangerous.

Sam turned his back on the creature and walked back to the driver's side door of the car. He heard no sounds, but suddenly the creature was there, right beside him. It moved much too fast to have walked or run toward him. Sam felt the beast pressing against his left elbow as he swung himself into the car seat. The beast touched the fabric of his shirt and seemed fascinated. Sam swung the door shut but the beast didn't leave. The car window was open and it leaned heavily on it. Sam felt the suspension system give under the tremendous weight of the beast. He thought of his tires like rubber balloons trying to absorb the pressure. "Listen, Biggie, you're going to bust my tires if you don't stop that."

The beast leaned in the car window and wheezed spittle all over Sam's face and neck as it studied him closely. Sam gagged at the terrible smell from the old beast's mouth. It smelled rotted. Sam's face felt wet from the spittle, but he dared not wipe it. Instead, he leaned forward and started the car. The beast pulled its upper torso out of the car as the engine turned over. It stood there bemused by the sudden rumble of the engine. It was not afraid and Sam gently shifted it into gear. He pressed down on the accelerator and eased the car forward a few feet before taking off. The beast did not act frightened in any way. Sam looked out of his rearview mirror as he drove off and saw it standing heavily and watching the car's red taillights wink away. The beast's one arm was extended outward as if in a final wave. Sam would never encounter the beast again.

Most of the traits Sam Sherry described were very typical for a Bigfoot. The sounds, the smells, the weight, and the curiosity were all common attributes. The almost teleporting movements and some other physical features, however, were not typical.

Johnson researched Sam's sighting, and he and Sam became good friends. Sam's experience made him more curious about the beasts and he became a researcher himself, often working with Johnson. Sam Sherry figured largely in several other Bigfoot adventures in Pennsylvania, but his desire to learn about the creature began on a cool spring night with a very close encounter.

The Deer Killer Case

In 1972, the motion picture *The Legend of Boggy Creek* was released in theaters. In one scene, a woman sits in her house with her back to a window while a large, hairy, heavy-breathing creature watches her from outside. Suddenly, the eerie silence is broken by the crash of glass and the terrified screams of the young woman as the beast's arm comes toward her through the broken window. If you describe that scene at a Bigfoot conference, many of the attendees will smile and tell you that that film is what got them started on cryptid research. The fact of the matter is that there is something deep inside of us that warns us to be afraid of Bigfoot. Yes, the creatures can by shy and retiring, but there are other tales that few tell of a more aggressive creature. The next few stories offer glimpses of the more dangerous Bigfoot.

The northern part of Pennsylvania still has a great deal of untamed wilderness. There are areas where deer outnumber the humans, and folks up there like it that way. As peaceful as this sounds, living in such a rural setting has some disadvantages that most people don't often think about. There are a great number of wild things on the loose in this rugged land, and some folks say that Bigfoot is among them. The names of the witnesses in this story have been changed at their request.

The Fourth of July 2006 was a lovely hot summer's day. The Smith family celebrated the way that most Americans do. They enjoyed a picnic with family and friends and then watched the local fireworks show. The family consisted of father, mother, and their teenage son and daughter. It was quite late when the family arrived home that night. They were happy, sleepy, and totally unprepared for what was about to occur.

Mr. Smith parked the car and everyone tumbled out. Picnic hampers and blankets were quickly unloaded from the car. The family started up the driveway to the house. Suddenly from the woods that surrounded them they heard a scream. They thought it was an animal's loud cry, but it made the hair at the back of their necks stand on end. It was frightening. The Smiths paused, looking at the woods to see what was there in the darkness. Suddenly, another cry came from a different direction. They turned and then a third cry came from yet another direction. The Smiths were puzzled.

Mr. Smith led the family around to the backyard, where the hamper was laid down. From the woods came more cries. It was certain they were hearing three different cries from three different creatures. The screams grew extremely loud and the family froze, looking into the darkness and trying to decipher what was going on. Then Mrs. Smith unlocked the back door and they all hurried into the house.

The Smiths discussed what they heard. Mr. Smith later described the cries as the screams King Kong made in the movies. They were all sure these were the sounds of large animals. They were also all in agreement that there had to have been at least three different creatures in the woods because the cries came from different places, almost as if they were answering each other.

The Smiths had lived in their home in the woods for some time and had never heard such sounds before. Mr. Smith wanted to investigate what was outside, but he decided to wait until morning. He didn't want to face whatever could make that sound alone in the darkness.

The next day, the family took a walk in the woods. They were curious to see if they could find any traces of the beasts from the night before. They walked across the field behind their house and into the woods. They walked around the property, circling it in the trees. It was then that they made their grisly discovery. Wedged in the crotch of a tree was the upper torso of a deer. The poor animal had died a brutal death. Its right front leg had been wedged into the tree crotch and wrenched around. Then it had been hit in the head with a rock. The back half of the deer was gone. It looked as if it had literally been torn in half by brute force.

The Smiths then found large, bare footprints, similar to those of a human, only much larger. They had no doubt that a large humanoid, or several, had been trampling the area the night before. They also saw the rock that had been used to strike the deer. It was covered with hair and blood. There were uprooted saplings and limbs broken off of larger trees. Something violent had torn through the area. It was enough to frighten the family alone in the woods.

It was not hard for the Smiths to leap to the idea of Bigfoot creatures in their woods. Mr. and Mrs. Smith found a Web site for the Pennsylvania Bigfoot Society, contacted the group, and told them their story. Within days, a team arrived at the Smith home and secured the site. There had been no rain during that time, so the prints, blood, and other evidence remained much as it had been that first day. The team accompanied the Smiths to the site and took photographs of everything there. They immediately recognized the tree-twisting and breaking as a little-known, but common, trait of Bigfoot. Although the Smiths had been unaware of it at the time, Bigfoot creatures were believed to have run deer to the ground and killed them before.

The research team examined the deer kill and found the guts all intact except for the heart and liver, which were both missing. These protein-rich organs seemingly are always missing from suspected Bigfoot kills.

The team's conclusion was that the deer had died from blunt-force trauma to the head caused by the blows with a rock. There were no signs of human interaction at the site. There were no bullet holes, casings, or arrow marks found near the site. The deer was torn, not cut in half, and was either placed in the tree before or just after death. They noted that there is only one creature in Pennsylvania's history that would place a kill in a tree—a mountain lion, now extinct in the state. They climb up into the tree with their kill, however, to eat it.

As a postscript to this bizarre tale, the family remembered a series of events that had happened a few months before the strange deer kill. Early in the spring of the same year, a friend had come to visit. The friend stayed in an RV on the property rather than in the house with the family. Early in the morning hours one night, the man was startled awake by something pounding and shaking the RV. Whatever the creature was, it had managed to shake the RV violently, requiring great size and strength. The friend sat in the RV for the rest of the night, waiting for the assailant to return. When daylight dawned, he went into the main house and told the family about his strange and terrifying night and said he was leaving immediately.

The team returned to the Smith home and the site of the deer kill case many times. They further noted that nothing ever touched the deer carcass. It remained in the tree for a long time. The bones and fur remained, but it is still a terrifying reminder of the strength and brutality of those creatures that stalked the woods near the Smiths' home not so long ago.

The Murderous Monster of Brier Hill

Financially, the loss of cattle, pigs, or horses can be a significant hardship to a farmer. Imagine how upset the farmers between Brier Hill and Masontown, Erie County, were when they were visited by the Murderous Monster of Brier Hill in the fall of 1926.

When the first farmer reported that something had broken into his chicken coop and killed a number of good hens, it was shrugged off as just the price of being a farmer. The farmer was shocked to see that many of the chickens were partly devoured. No fox or dog could be at fault for this carnage. Could anything other than a very large animal eat so much?

Within days, other chicken coops were attacked. On several farms, pigsties were breeched and something had literally pulled apart and devoured half-grown hogs. Pets and farm animals alike were being killed and torn apart at an alarming rate.

Some folks muttered that the circus in Brownsville had been the scene of a gorilla escape, but that was never proven. Gorillas, of course, would have no reason to slaughter and consume dozens upon dozens of animals, because they are largely herbivores.

Families in the area began to grow nervous. They believed that some very large creature was to blame and they gave it a name, "The Murderous Monster of Brier Hill." Anything large enough to kill a hog could kill a child or possibly even an adult. Parents in the area no longer allowed their children out to play. What if the "monster" was lurking? Young women began to feel a bit nervous, too. The entire area began to feel that it was under siege.

Then a farmer came into town to report another animal mutilation. This time the animals were a cow and a horse on the same farm. Both animals appeared to have struggled mightily with their attacker. Both were found disemboweled and pulled apart by raw force. No one saw the great beast that had committed so many killings, but it was not for lack of trying. Armed posses went out to search for clues after each killing. On at least two occasions, blood trails from dead chickens led to Brier Hill, but there was not a clue to the identity of the murderous creature.

Chickens seemed to be a particular favorite, and the birds were often found with their heads ripped off and torn to pieces. Why would any creature do something so vicious? Other chickens were carried away and the partly eaten remains were found, but nothing gave a clue to the identity of the culprit.

After several weeks of carnage, the beast seemed to move on. To this day, no one has been able to figure out exactly what type of being visited Brier Hill in the fall of 1926.

The beast may have returned briefly in 1938. A thirteen-year-old girl and two smaller children were horrified by a "furry thing resembling an ape" that gave chase to them briefly on the girl's family farm. Whatever the beast was, it appeared to be only about four feet tall and very strong. This creature may have had nothing to do with the earlier attacks, since nothing was killed this time, but folks had long memories and wondered if the two events could have been connected.

The Strange Thing that Happened to Joe

In 1980, the James Young family lived in a mobile home near the woods in rugged Williamson Township, Cambria County. The family was not concerned about what was in the woods near their rural home. They were not interested in monsters and Bigfoot. They cared about work, family, and their dogs.

On a Friday night in August 1980, Jim awoke at about 1:30 A.M. to the sound of his three hunting dogs and his German shepherd pup, Joe, barking wildly. The dogs were used to the normal night sounds and smells of the woodland, so Jim thought someone might be messing around on the property. He got dressed and slipped outside to see what was happening.

The cool night air felt good to Jim after the oppressive heat of the August day, but he had no time to enjoy it. As Jim stood behind his home looking around, strange high-pitched screams and low growls and grunts disturbed the night. It didn't quite sound human, Jim thought as he frantically racked his brain for any idea of what the creature could be. Heavy wheezy breathing filled the air. Suddenly, a terrible stench came wafting toward Jim across the breeze. It was one of the foulest things he had ever smelled, and Jim nearly gagged. It was like rank body odor, human waste, and a strange musky scent all combined. There was an acrid odor to it, as well, reminding Jim of the air at the coal mines not far away. The smell was terrible!

Jim glanced around at the woods where the dogs were directing their barks. He saw nothing, but the strange cries still came occasionally and the hair on Jim's neck stood up. It was as if he had caught the fear from the dogs. Jim checked to make sure that the dogs were safely tied, and then he turned his attention to the half-grown German shepherd pup, Joe. The dog usually roamed free, but now Jim caught it by the collar and tried to figure out what to do with the dog. He couldn't have a dog attacking someone. The smell suddenly faded, and the sounds stopped. The dogs then calmed down. Jim let go of Joe's collar and the dog dropped to his feet, but he growled low under his breath, as if not quite satisfied that whatever had been out there was really gone.

Jim went back inside and lay back down. Although he was tired, he could not help but wonder what the dogs had sensed. What type of creature made sounds like that, and what about that terrible stench? Later that day, Jim was no longer concerned about what had happened in the early morning hours. Whatever the creature was, it had surely passed on during the night.

That night, Saturday, Jim again found himself awakened by the sound of the dogs yapping. He pulled on some pants and walked outside. It was a night much like the previous one and Jim almost felt a sense of déjà vu. The hound dogs were baying toward the woods and pulling on their chains anxiously. Joe was growling low and tensed as if waiting for something.

The smell hit Jim first this time. It was that terrible stench of the night before. Jim gagged as he scanned the tree line for motion, but he saw nothing. Then the beast gave out a cry and Jim turned toward the sound. The moonlight on the shadows made it hard to see until Jim's eyes adjusted. A bright moon lit the world well and suddenly something shifted in the darkness of the tree line. Joe snapped and lunged forward, breaking away from Jim. Jim tried to capture the dog, but it was too fast and too strong. The shadowy something turned and crashed through the brush with a whining cry. Joe launched himself forward into the woods. Jim called to the dog, but it ignored him. For a long time Jim called for Joe before accepting that the dog was gone. The other dogs settled back down and Jim finally went inside. In the morning, he went looking for Joe, but did not want to be caught alone in the darkness with the thing that stunk so bad. It was as if an instinct told him to be wary. Jim decided to call his brother, a lieutenant in the local police force. Jim's brother would bring the situation to the attention of the local police.

It was late morning before Jim saw Joe again. His brash, aggressive German shepherd lay whimpering near the edge of the woods. At first Jim thought that the dog was hurt, but an examination proved that was not the case. Joe was fine physically, but he was one terrified dog. Jim tied the half-grown shepherd and waited for the police.

When the police arrived, they were shocked to see how cowered Joe was. Only a week before, an officer had been put back in his car by the same dog. Now all of the spirit was gone from the beast. Something traumatic had happened to Joe.

Sunday morning Jim was awakened by his two sons, Jimmy and Frank, who had been roused by the dogs. The boys had gone outside to see what was disturbing them and they had heard rough, ragged breathing. The boys got scared, because whatever creature was breathing so loudly had to be very big. They had gone to awaken their dad.

Jim turned the lights on and the three went out to look for the creature that was scaring the dogs. Joe was whimpering as if he were about to be killed. He slunk back into his box with his tail between his legs. Seeing the condition of the dog frightened the family, who were still shocked at the difference in his personality.

It was then that the same putrid, acidic smell filled the damp morning air and Jim hurried back inside to call the police. There really wasn't much that could be done, however, for no one had committed any crimes and no one was proven to be in danger.

Around 9:30 A.M., Jim went outside to tend to his animals. He had rabbits in pens built off the ground, and it was then that he got a shock. On the far side of the rabbit pens, only yards from the dog's area, there was one perfect footprint in the mud. The print looked human in shape and had five toes, but was much too large and heavy to be human. The heel of the print went $3^3/4$ inches down into the soft dirt. Eight feet further out, a partial second print was seen. It had a tremendous stride. The prints were $17^1/2$ inches across. Jim again called the police. They made a cast of the print and later surmised that a creature of unknown origin had crossed the Young family's yard at an angle. It went past the dog pens and jumped over the rabbit pens. It was then that the deep imprint was made. The beast then hurried on its way, leaving the agitated animals behind along with one more partial print.

For weeks the police combed the area looking for the creature. They never found a Bigfoot or another print, but there were those who lived through the experience who didn't need proof. It appeared that a Bigfoot, who may have spent time in the old mines, was living in the area. There was little doubt that something terrible had happened to Joe. The dog would recover somewhat, but he'd never again be the brash dog of his puppyhood.

The Strange Wild Man

Something strange had been stalking the farms in Lancaster County in the early winter of 1858. Farmers were shocked to find that their cattle were not only stripped of milk, but that the animals were reacting as if terrified of something unknown. Other farmers found smaller livestock dead and blood drained from the animals.

Folks in Lancaster County were shocked when a farmer claimed to have finally sighted the culprit. The farmer said he was going to his barn one day when he was knocked aside by a large creature. He claimed that it was a hairy man. This man was covered with dark hair all over his body and was very strong. The wild man smelled bad and gave out shrill screams.

Soon, another farmer reported seeing a similar creature. Then another farmer came forward with the same story. He said the "wild man" entered his barn and he was shocked to see him on the ground sucking milk directly from the teats of the distressed cow.

The wild man sprang forward and turned as if to rush the farmer, but then he jumped the stall and ran off without hurting him. The farmer said that the man was naked and covered in black hair. He ran very fast upright, never dropping on all fours.

Skeptics reasoned that the farmers were dealing with a black bear, but those who actually saw the beast insisted that it was something like a wild man or a gorilla. At that time the word "Bigfoot" had not yet been coined, but it seems in many ways to fit the Classic Bigfoot description.

Bizarre Bigfoot

Beyond Classic Bigfoot, we enter a realm of other hominid creatures that are rarely reported. Bigfoot creatures that shift in and out of this dimension, smaller creatures, and several different types of Bigfoot creatures are all represented in this rarely before discussed facet of cryptozoology.

In 1973 and 1974, Pennsylvania became known nationally for the many strange Bigfoot and UFO events occurring simultaneously. Not only were there an unusually large number of events, but they were very strange stories. Floating creatures, disappearing creatures, and bizarre UFO and Bigfoot combined events took place throughout the state. This chapter offers a sampling of the strange events that occurred in Pennsylvania during that time.

Bigfoot and the Mysterious Sphere

On a hot August evening in 1973, a family in Beaver County experienced one of the strangest encounters ever recorded in Pennsylvania. It all began when the two teenage girls of the family were walking through the woods near their home. The girls heard sounds in the brush as if something large was moving through the woods. They stopped and looked around, and to their surprise, they saw a large white creature moving through the forest.

The beast was like a hairy man or ape. The girls later estimated that it was about eight feet tall. It walked upright with the stride of a human, but also had some apelike features. It had red eyes.

The beast was carrying a glowing sphere in its hand. The sphere was emitting a soft light, and the beast was staring at it intensely as it walked along. The entire event was traumatizing for the girls, and they quickly turned and fled the woods after the beast disappeared among the trees.

The girls were as quiet as possible until they burst out into their own yard. There they took off running for the house. They found their parents and told them their strange story. The parents didn't know what to make of the fanciful tale, but they did realize that the girls must have seen something, because they were truly upset. The father decided to get to the bottom of the mystery by checking out the woods for himself.

Hours passed and darkness slipped across the land. The horrified little family waited for the father to return and tried to decide if they should call the police. The mother was determined that if she didn't hear something soon, she'd risk looking foolish and call the police.

At last the father came stumbling across the yard. He was very confused and couldn't remember much after entering the woods. He remembered the girls' story and setting out to get to the bottom of things, but what happened after he entered the woods was a blank to him. He was shocked by the amount of time that had elapsed. He thought that only moments had gone by when in reality it had been hours.

The father began to suffer from the psychological effects of his blackout. He found himself compelled to go back to the location frequently, but he never recalled the missing time—at least publicly.

Beauty and the Bigfoot

In September 1973, a woman in the Whitney area of West-moreland County decided to visit the graves of her loved ones at St. James Cemetery. She took along her three-year-old daughter, who played nearby as the woman tended to the graves.

The afternoon passed quickly. It was nearly dusk by the time the woman finished at the cemetery. The little girl sat on the grass playing for quite a while and then toddled off. Her mother let her roam a bit, because it was a small cemetery and the child could do no harm.

Suddenly, the woman felt a shift in the atmosphere around her. She got the feeling she was being watched. She glanced around sharply and saw her little girl playing peacefully in the grass at a distance. Then she saw it. Coming out of the shadows of the trees was a large, hairy bipedal creature. The beast had dark hair all over his body, and he was intently watching the woman as he inched closer to the child.

The little girl saw the creature and stood up. Her mother called softly for the child, but the little girl did not heed her mother's call. Instead, she toddled off directly toward the beast. The mother gasped and ran toward the little girl. She grabbed up the child and hustled her toward the car. The beast stood still and simply watched the woman's frantic movements. With the child in the car, the mother gunned the engine and left the beast behind.

The woman was understandably rattled by her experience. Things would get stranger during the next few days when the neighbors began reporting the appearance of a strange, hairy creature lurking around the family's home. The woman lived more than five miles from the cemetery, and it was quite unnerving for her to think that the beast had followed her. The family was so rattled by the events that they later called in researchers. An examination of the cemetery did not reveal any evidence of the creature, but the eyewitnesses were adamant about their story. Researchers spoke to the witnesses and gathered their accounts, but found no physical evidence at the places where the creature was encountered.

The Goose-stealing Bigfoot

Bigfoot researchers were kept busy by the varied and vast encounters with Bigfoot and UFOs throughout the state in the early 1970s. From alien abductions to Bigfoot attacks, the state seemed inundated with the bizarre. In the Lancaster area, a strange report was filed with the local police by a farmwoman. She reported that she had been out in her barnyard feeding the chickens and other birds when a large, hairy creature came swooping out of the woods toward her. It moved fast and the woman had no time to react before the beast was upon her. But it didn't attack her. Instead, it grabbed two large pet geese from the barnyard and began to make off with them.

The woman reacted before she could think and gave chase while screaming for help. The geese honked and hissed as they attempted to escape. The beast ran on two legs like a human, but it was taller than the average man and broader built.

The beast was evidently upset by the woman challenging it. It turned around and threw one of the geese at the woman. The bird hit her in the chest hard enough to knock her down. The beast escaped with the remaining goose, while the woman struggled to get to her feet again after having had the breath knocked out of her.

The woman would later contact Bigfoot researchers with her story. By the time she thought to do so, however, all possible evidence was gone. The woman didn't need researchers to tell her what she saw, though. She was most upset about the encounter and the loss of her pet.

Beach Hill Bigfoot

A couple we will call the Jacksons sat on their porch one hot night in August 1973 watching the evening sky and enjoying the first cool breezes of evening. As the Jacksons talked, they noticed something strange in the sky above their Beach Hill home near Greensburg. Mrs. Jackson was the first to see the object in the sky.

As she watched, a boomerang-shaped object loomed up in the sky over the woods. The object seemed to hover over the woods and Mrs. Jackson called out for her husband to look over the trees. Mr. Jackson looked and jumped up. Not only did he see the craft hovering over the woods, he could have sworn that he also saw a large, hairy creature watching them from the tree line.

Mr. Jackson ran into the house and called for his wife to follow. He got a rifle and hurried back outside. He ran toward the tree line to see the creature better. He later reported that the creature had long thick hair and walked on two legs like a man. It showed no evidence of fearing Mr. Jackson. He was able to approach it at point-blank range and pull off a shot. The beast did not so much as flinch.

The creature moved on as if nothing had happened. The Jacksons later reported the experience to the Pennsylvania Center for UFO Research. This would only be one of many strange co-encounters with UFOs and Bigfoot creatures in the state between 1973 and 1974. The exact nature of the encounter has never been determined.

Bigfoot Lands in a UFO

On October 25, 1973, Stephen Pulaski and a group of fifteen other folks from two farms watched a bright red ball hovering high above a field on the Pulaski farm in the Greensburg area.

Stephen was twenty-two years old and stood six foot two. He was very curious about the mysterious light, but at that time no one was unduly frightened or upset about it. Stephen decided to drive up into the field for a better look. A neighbor's ten-year-old twin boys accompanied him. Stephen took along a loaded 30.06 rifle in case of trouble.

As the truck drew closer to the red ball, the headlights began to dim. At the same time, the red ball began to move. It came down directly into the field. Although, Stephen wouldn't know it until later, his dog back at the house grew increasingly agitated at this time and went wild.

Up in the field, Stephen and the boys watched as the red ball changed to white. Now Stephen could see that the object was approximately one hundred feet in diameter. Stephen said "It was dome-shaped, just like a big bubble." The machine made a sound like a lawn mower, but he saw no engine.

Stephen and the twins got out of the truck to better observe the craft. Suddenly, one of the twins called out that there was something moving along the fence line. Stephen attempted to focus, but he was nearsighted and it was difficult to see in the darkness. He could make out two figures and he fired a tracer round well over their heads. He could not see the figures clearly, but he could tell that they were not people. They were way too large and strangely proportioned, but he could see they were bipeds. They were standing by six-foot-tall fence posts, so that enabled Stephen to estimate that one figure was seven feet and the other was a foot taller. His first thought was that they were bears reared up, because they were covered in gray fur. As the creatures moved, Stephen caught a better look at them. Their eyes had a green-gold glow. They were decidedly not human.

Stephen and the boys later described to the police and researchers that the larger creature ran its hands over the fence posts as it moved along. The smaller one seemed to take abnormally long, fast strides, as if to keep up with the larger beast.

The boys agreed that the creatures' arms hung nearly to the ground. Both beasts were making "whining sounds," almost like a baby. The two creatures seemed to be talking back and forth as they hurried along. Stephen and the boys noticed a burned rubber smell.

Stephen raised the gun and fired a second time, both out of fear and because the creatures were now slowly approaching them. The bullet did not seem to deter the creatures. In a panic, Stephen fired into the larger creature three times. One of the boys turned and ran back toward the farmhouse, leaving his brother with Stephen.

Stephen later told authorities that he was sure he hit the creature, because it gave out a whining sound and then reached out toward the other creature. At the same moment, the white bubble craft simply vanished. The beasts turned and walked back toward the woods slowly. A white glow began to emanate from where the craft had been. It was a light "so bright that you could read a newspaper by it," according to Stephen. His eyes began to burn and hurt. He and the remaining child turned and got back into the truck. They headed back to the farmhouse, where they found the other twin winded and terrified.

The two families were shocked by what the three told them. They all wanted to call the police, particularly since a gun had been fired, but Stephen was reluctant at first. He then agreed that he should tell the authorities what they had witnessed.

The first police officer to respond to the call was a Pennsylvania State Police trooper named Byrne. He arrived about 9:45 P.M. Byrne listened to the strange story and decided that they should investigate. He convinced Stephen that he had to go along to show him where the events took place.

Byrne drove Stephen up the dirt road to the field. They parked approximately a hundred yards away from where the light was still glowing. At this point, it looked like a bubble of transparent light. Byrne left his car idling and the headlights on.

The trooper first examined the glowing bubble of light. It was bright enough that Stephen noticed that the flashlight beam sort of faded into it. Byrne then began to explore the field and woods with the light as he walked toward the area. They walked along the row near the electric fence and suddenly froze. Approximately fifty feet away, in the woods, came the sound of heavy footsteps.

Whatever was moving in their direction, it had no intention of being quiet. They could hear branches snapping and young trees being torn out of the ground. The creature sounded like it was on a rampage. The two men moved further away from the area, but the noise followed them. Again they moved and the creature seemed to alter its course to follow them. They hurried back toward the safety of the car.

Byrne and Stephen talked a few moments, calmed down, and observed the area. They decided to try investigating one more time and got out of the car. They moved a little distance from it when Stephen froze. Something terrified him. He wanted to leave the area.

"I don't get paid to be brave," he told the trooper. "I'm not going any further." Byrne later said that his greatest worry was for the safety of Stephen. He felt that Stephen needed to get away from the situation, so they turned back to the car. Before getting inside, the officer reached to turn off his headlights for a second to see if the area was still glowing. At that moment, Stephen saw a brown mass moving toward them and he cried out that they needed to shoot it. Byrne allowed him to take the shot. It was Stephen's last bullet.

Stephen's hands were shaking. He was pale and the officer began to worry for him. Then Stephen saw movement in the woods. Something was moving toward them rapidly. Both men jumped into the car and took off. The trooper caught himself about fifty feet down the dirt road and turned the car around. They were safe in the car, he reasoned, and they needed to remain calm. They waited a few moments, but they neither saw nor heard anything else.

The trooper later made several interesting observations. He said that the light rose up from the ground about a foot. He could see plants by it and it might have been warmer near the light, but he wasn't sure. He did notice that the cattle and horses in the field did not want to be anywhere near the area. The dogs were agitated and upset. Stephen later said that the light winked out as they turned the car around. The officer didn't observe the light disappearing.

Back at the farmhouse, Byrne said that he'd return to the barracks and phone a paranormal investigator named Stan Gordon who might be able to help.

Byrne called Gordon, who gathered a research team and drove directly to the site. They arrived at the farm at 1:30 A.M. In addition to Gordon, the researchers included Bob McCurry, George Lutz, Dennis Smeltzer, Dave Baker, and Dave Smith. They found a very anxious group of people at the house. The research team wanted to go up to the field immediately. Stephen had to be persuaded to take the team up. The boys and Stephen's German shepherd rode along.

The ring of light was no longer visible. The investigators checked for radiation, but there were no elevated levels. Stephen's father had joined the group, and while the team was searching, he and Stephen stayed at the truck with the children. Suddenly, they began to yell. The farmhouse had just lit up and was literally glowing. The rest of the team did not see the glow, but they sent George Lutz and Stephen's father to check on the house. When they got there, all was fine.

Then a bull at the far side of the field began to bellow and back away as if frightened by something. At nearly the same instant, Stephen's dog started barking and growling at the edge of the woods near the field. The group studied the area, but did not see movement.

George Lutz and Stephen's father returned. George was talking to Stephen when he noticed Stephen rubbing his head and face. George asked Stephen if he was alright. Stephen looked at George almost uncertainly and began to teeter on his feet. He collapsed as his father caught him on one side and George caught him on the other side. Stephen's breathing was heavy and ragged. Within seconds, he was shaking his head and growling deep in his throat like an animal. Stephen weighed nearly 250 pounds, so he was difficult to hold. His arms swung wildly, shaking off George and his father. The German shepherd lunged at Stephen as if to attack his master. Stephen lunged back at the dog and the dog began to run away yipping. Stephen chased after it, growling and ready to attack. George and Mr. Pulaski ran after Stephen and called to him to come back.

Stan Gordon and his team had turned toward the commotion. Before anyone could react, Dennis Smeltzer suddenly cried out, "Hey, Stan, I'm starting to feel lightheaded." He began to have difficulty breathing.

As Stan and the team tried to care for Dennis and keep an eye on Stephen, Stephen suddenly stopped. He looked blankly at the group and then collapsed face-first into a patch of cow manure. He was unconscious.

As the team began to take care of Stephen, he came around and began to cry out. "Get away from me! It's here. Get back! Get back!" At that moment, most of the group sensed a strong smell of sulfur. George called out that they should leave the area immediately.

Stephen cried out. "Keep away from the corner! It's in the corner!" He was being supported by his father who had been leading him down the hill at the time.

Stephen kept moving forward toward the farmhouse, but he was muttering about wanting to protect everyone. He muttered about seeing a man "in a black hat and cloak, carrying a sickle." This man was talking to Stephen, and Stephen relayed the message to the team. "If man doesn't straighten up, the end will come soon," Stephen said. "There is a man here now who can save the world." Then Stephen said that the man was calling his name over and over. "Stephen! Stephen! Stephen!" Stephen insisted that the figure making him hear the voice was back in the woods.

As they neared the house, Stephen began to act normally again. He did not have any history of seizures, hallucinations or psychic phenomena. He never took any medication for mental illness. After that night Stephen began to take nerve medication. He took it for years afterward.

The research team later stated that Stephen seemed to be suffering from contactee syndrome. *Contactee syndrome* was a term coined to explain a condition suffered by those who have encountered or been abducted by aliens. Common in these interactions are messages about the future, man's peril, and warnings that the earth and mankind are in jeopardy. The researchers felt that Stephen should seek medical treatment and helped him find professionals to deal with his stress over his experiences on the farm that night.

The Apple Barrel Raider

There have been stories of the strange creatures we call Bigfoot stealing fruit from the natives ever since the first white man came along to record the tales. Imagine the surprise that a woman in Indiana, Pennsylvania, had when she encountered a strange pilferer.

The bounty of fall ends with the blush of red and gold that is apple-picking time. For many rural folks, gathering apples is an end-of-summer tradition. They gather them carefully, so as not to bruise them, and then tuck them away safely in root cellars and basements to await cold weather. One woman in Indiana County had gathered the last of the fall apples and had stored them in a barrel on her front porch. She thought that she'd have her adult son move them to other quarters when he had a chance, but as the nights were cool, she was not worried that the apples would spoil quickly in the barrel.

Early on the morning of September 13, 1973, the woman got up and went downstairs to begin her day. She soon became aware of a strange sound of something dropping or thudding outside. The woman went to her front door and looked out expecting a raccoon or opossum. What she saw sent her running in shock. It was a large dark-haired bipedal creature eating apples. The sound of thudding was apples hitting the porch as the creature dug through the barrel. Bitten apples had been slung across the porch.

The woman made a sound and the beast looked up sharply, but then it returned to tasting the juicy fruit. The woman made a dash up to her son's room. He got out of bed, grabbed his gun, and rushed downstairs. When he threw open the front door, he could barely believe his eyes. The apelike creature had replaced the lid on the barrel and was sitting on it happily munching an apple. The beast stood up abruptly and took off running. The young man got off two shots at the creature at almost point-blank range. He later told investigators that he was sure that he hit the beast, but it showed no signs of being shot. It simply kept on running and disappeared into the woods.

Red Eyes

Near the town of Kinston in Luzerne County on August 17, 1973, a man was driving along when he had a shocking encounter. A large, hairy creature ran out in the road in front of him. The man swerved and missed the beast. The driver was badly shaken as he watched the beast before him run into the brush and disappear.

The driver contacted the police and told them the beast was a large, hairy biped, but it was not an ordinary Bigfoot creature either. He describes this beast as "gorilla-like." The beast had pointed ears and red eyes that glowed with infernal light. The beast seemed enraged by the near-accident and let out bellowing screams that were incredibly human in sound and quality. The screams reminded the driver of a man crying out in severe pain.

The Disappearing Bigfoot

It was a cold night in February when a woman in her late fifties, who here will be called Norma, heard rattling sounds on her back porch. Norma had lived her entire life in the woods of western Pennsylvania. She knew the area like the back of her hand and she knew what walked, stalked, and flew through the night around her old house.

Norma reached for a rifle that she had sitting in the corner of the kitchen. Outside the sounds of something tearing up her garbage came to her clearly. It was either raccoons or a pack of feral dogs that were roaming the area. Either way, Norma figured on breaking up their supper. There wasn't much that she hated more than picking up garbage strewn across her porch each morning. She had tried cans, plastic bins, and assorted other ways to store the trash, but whatever was getting into her garbage was smart and determined.

Norma rammed back the bolt on the rifle and made sure that the gun was loaded. She was going to blast a few shots over the heads of the miscreants tearing up her trash. Norma pulled open the back door near the kitchen sink as she raised the gun. For one horrifying second, Norma struggled to understand what she was seeing. A large, brown, hairy hominid was standing in her doorway. Norma pulled the trigger as the creature raised its arms. The beast gave a startled cry as the bullets hit it point-blank in the chest, and then suddenly it just winked out. The creature hadn't turned and run, it simply vanished before Norma's eyes.

Norma slammed the door shut and bolted it. Her heart was pounding and her brain and eyes were still working on accepting what had just happened as the phone rang. It was her daughter and son-in-law calling. They lived about two hundred yards away through a screen of trees and they had been startled by the sudden burst of gunshots. Norma was too rattled to do anything other than tell the truth. She explained it all and ended with silence after she insisted that the beast had simply vanished. Her son-in-law, Rob, took the phone from his wife.

"I'm coming over, mother," he told Norma. "I'll be right there."

Norma told Rob that she was okay, but he wasn't convinced. "I'll check things out," he insisted. Norma hung up the phone and loaded the rifle again. She stood by the locked back door waiting in case there was any need for her help.

Rob shouldered into his coat and pulled on gloves. It was bitterly cold outside and he knew enough to bundle up. He moved with the precision and the ease of a true outdoorsman. Within seconds, he picked up his own gun and told his wife to keep the door locked until he returned.

Rob stepped out into the biting cold. It was so cold that it almost hurt to breath, but Rob barely noticed as he stepped off his own front porch and began crunching down the driveway toward the path to his mother's house.

Rob saw and heard nothing until he was in the woods about midway between the two houses. Suddenly, he saw glowing eyes staring at him and there was a terrible scream. It was a strange mewling sound, like a cross between a person's bellow and a cat's cry. He swung toward the sound and saw a large black shape, darker than the night. Behind him came another cry, and he flipped around in that direction. Another scream filled the night air and Rob turned again. He saw large, dark shapes moving toward him. He saw glowing eyes and heard their cries. Whatever the creatures were, they were black and larger than a man. They appeared to be shaggy and their eyes glowed as they moved nearer to him. Rob began popping shots at the beasts as he turned and ran for Norma's home.

Norma heard the heavy pounding sounds of her son-in-law's feet on the planks of the porch and the terror in his voice as he cried out for her to open up. She slammed the bolt back on the door and flung it open as Rob tore into the house. His face was white with shock and fear. His eyes were wide and he was heaving for breath.

"What the crap were those things?" he demanded, as his mother-in-law locked the door tightly once more.

On the table sat a box of shells and Rob grabbed some to reload the gun as he caught his breath. He looked at his mother-in-law's face and realized that she was in shock, too. "Tell me exactly what's been happening here," he demanded as he tried to assume control.

Norma explained about the torn garbage and her wanting to shoot over the head of the creature or creatures that were tearing it up. She described what had been on her porch and how she had shot at it. She knew that she had hit the beast, because it was point-blank range, but the beast simply disappeared like a popped balloon.

The family was so rattled by the experience that they called for help. They ended up reporting the events to Bigfoot researchers. They would begin to consider that perhaps there were many different types of Bigfoot creatures and several explanations for what was occurring during that period.

Even today, the cases in western Pennsylvania in 1973 and 1974 baffle researchers and are often not discussed by those in the cryptozoological community. Many researchers don't want to discuss these cases that defy the standard belief that Bigfoot is a physical hominid that will be captured one day.

Other Strange Humanoid Creatures

I f you think Bigfoot is the strangest creature in Pennsylvania, then be prepared to be shocked. There are other bipedal beasts with human characteristics walking, stalking, and tromping through the state. The stories of these creatures fade far back into the mists of time and continue to this day.

The Ridge Road Monster

In the late 1960s, a couple whom we will call John and Martha Steele lived a rough and rugged existence in Blair County. John had always made a living from the sweat of his brow, but the winter months were often very tough for the family. They raised a large garden every summer and canned for the winter, but a family with five children does not live on vegetables alone. John always provided the family's meat by hunting. The family lived in the woods at the end of an old dirt road known locally as Ridge Road, and it was there that John usually hunted. There were plenty of rabbits, squirrels, and turkeys in the woods, but he liked hunting deer there best of all. Across the ridge were farms, and so the fat, corn-fed deer were a great treat to the family.

The first day of buck season is like a holiday for hunters in Pennsylvania and it has always been that way. The season begins the Monday after Thanksgiving, and so it is often cold and bitter. Hunters like it that way, however, because the snow helps them track and the cold will hold the meat and make it better to butcher. John started out early on the first morning of buck season wearing his heavy coveralls and a red jacket. He climbed a tree and watched for deer, hopeful that he'd be bringing home meat that day.

It was not a good day for hunters. A drizzle fell and made everything damp and stiff. The woods seemed devoid of all wildlife. John had never seen the woods so quiet and empty. The only sounds he heard were the dead leaves rustling along, tree branches thrashing in the wind, and the distant boom of guns as other hunters had more luck than he did.

By the afternoon, John was cold, hungry, and stiff. He felt discouraged and decided that he'd better get back home before darkness fell. It was already twilight under the trees and John shouldered his rifle before setting off. He was walking along the dirt track when he caught movement in the distance. He strained his eyes in the half light to see who was moving ahead of him. He could tell this person was not wearing hunting clothes. He called out in a friendly manner to the man, but he got no response. He wondered if the fellow hadn't heard him or if the man was ignoring him.

John called out again and waited, but the figure still wouldn't respond. As John walked along, he observed that the man was tall and thin, but something about his proportions was off. He moved like a stick figure, or a bag of bones, with jerky motions that didn't seem like a man's smooth strides. Suddenly, a gap opened up in the laced tree branches above and the figure stepped into the wedge of brighter light. John could not help the involuntary gasp as he saw the figure more clearly.

Whatever the thing before him was, it was now clear it was not a man. It was nude and its gray skin seemed stretched over a tall skeleton. It was more than seven feet tall and its arms swung down almost to its knees. But what terrified John was the beast's head. It looked like gray skin over a skull and nothing more. It turned and John could see cadaverous red eyes glowing. The red eyes were the only sign of life in the face.

The beast stared and John gripped his rifle tightly. He was frozen there in the middle of the road and dared not move lest the beast launch itself back at him. Instead, the beast turned away from John and stepped off the path into one of the many sinkholes that dotted the area and stood still. It raised its head as if to look at the sky and gave out a long, mournful wail that chilled John and sent shudders down his back. Then the beast started to sink into the hole as if being lowered somehow. The entire time it sank, it gave out the strange, hollow cries that made John's skin crawl.

John took off running and never stopped until he reached his home. He told his wife about the beast, but never told another soul. That was until about nine years later when his family would have one more encounter with the Ridge Road Monster.

The youngest of John and Martha's children was a twelve-year-old boy named David. David was given the job of feeding the dogs that lived in kennels near the edge of Ridge Road. John was working as the local dogcatcher at the time. He liked working with dogs, but he didn't enjoy having to put them down. That was how he had ended up with a multitude of dog boxes and dogs across from his house at the mouth of Ridge Road. John would try to find the dogs homes if he could. He also had his own dogs there, two hunting dogs and a large German shepherd named Bingo. David was to feed the dogs and water them twice a day. He didn't mind doing the task before school, but he hated going across the road at dusk to feed them once more. He always felt uneasy with the woods wrapped around him. He felt watched.

One night the dogs started a racket that caused John to question David if he had fed the dogs. David admitted that he hadn't done so, and his father admonished him to get out there and do the job immediately. The dogs barked, bayed, and howled as David hurried over with buckets full of feed and water. He moved systematically from one box to another and was grateful for the large pole light that stood at the edge of the compound. It provided a puddle of yellow light that pushed back the darkness.

Suddenly, the dogs all stopped barking except for Bingo. David looked around and realized that despite being fed, the dogs had all taken to their boxes. He could hear some faint whimpers from some of the boxes, but not another sound. Only Bingo continued to bark and he lunged against his bonds as if trying to reach something. David turned to see what had upset Bingo and dropped the feed bucket.

Standing below the pole light was a tall, gray creature, similar to what his father had seen. It was emaciated with bones protruding out and covered by gray flesh. Its head was skeletal and it had red, glowing eyes. David took off running toward the house and screaming.

John and Martha took some time to calm down the terrified boy. David was sure that he'd be chastised for letting the work at the dog pens unfinished, but his parents were amazingly kind about the situation. It was then that David heard about his father's own experience with the creature.

As long as the family lived at the end of Ridge Road, they would not venture out into the darkness at night. They preferred to drive the ridge rather than walk it, even by daylight. They never saw the beast again, but they all knew that something was out there, something that they couldn't explain.

John and Martha have since passed away and the property is no longer owned by the family. Both ends of Ridge Road now have families living on them. Interestingly, some of those families have reported hearing strange cries from the woods in the area. One family even claims to have seen the beast and photographed the creature. Unfortunately, the photo is now lost. Perhaps one of the most interesting accounts of the beast in recent times came from a farmer on the far side of the ridge who said that both he and his adult son have seen the beast on separate occasions standing at the edge of the woods at dusk, watching them work in the bordering fields.

There are other places where such creatures have been sighted. Ghost hunter Elliott O'Donnell once wrote about encountering such a beast in the Hudson Valley at the turn of the twentieth century. In South America, they describe similar beasts and view them as earth spirits. Whatever this creature is, it has always maintained a distance from humans, although it does seem to be a bit curious about what we're up to in its domain.

Encounter with an Albatwitch

Most folks in Pennsylvania are aware of the large, hairy creatures known as Bigfoot, but few realize there are also little beasts that stand about five foot tall. These were called "Albatwitches" in the Susquehannock language of the natives of Lancaster County.

The natives warned European settlers of the small, aggressive creatures that were known to steal from the camps and even pelt people with stones or apples. The name Albatwitch means "apple picker" or "apple snitcher" in the language of the Susquehannock.

Chickies Rock Park in Lancaster County has long been a popular destination for outings. The rock that leans out over the water is supposedly haunted, and was also a favorite spot for Albatwitches. It is said that they were once quite numerous in that region and had to be driven out by the Europeans and natives.

Old stories and legends are fine, but in February 2002, Rick Fisher was driving along Route 23 around 6:00 A.M. when he became aware of something moving ahead of him. As he approached it, he thought it was a human, so he began to slow down. Why on earth would someone be walking up the middle of the road in the darkness?

As Rick drew closer, he could see from the size of the figure that it was small. He thought perhaps it was a child. But why would a child be out on the road at that time of day?

Rick was now barely crawling along in the car. He flashed his lights on high beam to get the child's attention. When the figure turned around, it blinked and Rick saw that it had yellow glowing eyes. The light gave Rick a good look at the figure and he realized that whatever this thing was, it was not human. It stood about three feet tall and was covered with black hair. It didn't seem distressed. Then the small black beast simply vanished.

Rick pulled the car over and sat there shaking. He got out, but then it dawned on him that if it could wink out from the road, it might be able to materialize someplace else . . . like beside him or in the car.

Rick got back in and hurried away from the spot. He didn't tell anyone about his experience for some time, but at last he confided in a colleague at work. To Rick's great surprise, his colleague told him that he knew someone else who had seen the same thing just down the road a few miles from where Rick had seen the being.

Rick later began researching the subject and learned about Albatwitches. He found out that others in the area have had experiences with the creatures in recent years as well.

Attack of the Strange Fanged Creature

Lancaster County is known for its pastoral landscape and the large Amish population that lives there. The Amish are known for their unusual religious practices, sturdy work ethic, and strong family and community values, but they typically don't get involved with monster stories. In 1973, however, two Amish farmers had a strange story to tell that became part of the cryptozoological fabric of this state.

It was late summer and the farmers had been cutting hay and hauling it to the barns all day long. Cutting hay is hot, tiring work, and by evening they were both exhausted and glad to feel the cooler air. As the two men paused to rest between carrying loads of hay, they allowed the team of horses to also rest as well.

The two men passed the time for a few minutes and listened. They could hear children playing at the farmhouse close by. Suddenly, the tired horses began to start and fuss. The farmers turned to see what was wrong with them. That was when they heard a ruckus near the chicken coops and looked up to see a very strange sight. A large, hairy gray animal was running toward the chickens on two legs, just as a man would run. The beast was not far away, and they could see it clearly. It had a white mane around its neck that waved in the breeze, its teeth were protruding out like fangs, and it had horns that curved like a ram's. The beast caught sight of them and made a dash for a hen. The hapless hen gave out a startled squawk as it was snatched up by the beast's claws, which the farmers said looked like those of a grizzly bear. The beast stole the chicken and ran off.

The farmers struggled to keep the spooked team from running and had no chance to save the chicken. They were so rattled by what they had witnessed that they contacted the authorities to report it. The beast was not sighted again in the area, but this strange report has puzzled cryptozoologists for years.

The Yellow What-Is-It

The townships of Ruscombmanor and Muhlenberg in eastern Berks County were agog in October 1879 with strange tales. A mysterious beast had taken up residence in the area and was causing quite a stir. It all began early in the month when the son of the prison inspector came running into the little town of Topton Station raging about having seen a monster. He raced into the main hotel in town and told his tale to the hotel owner, O. Hinnershitz. Hinnershitz believed the young man. Several local fellows, in fact, decided to go looking for the beast.

There had already been stories afoot that a strange creature had been spotted in the countryside outside of town, but now Schmehl, the prison inspector's son, insisted that he had seen a yellow beast lying down near the gate to a local field only a little while earlier. Schmehl had been driving a herd of cattle into the field, and it was during this occupation that he had seen the beast. He described it as a yellow, mud-covered creature about four feet tall. It had long arms with only two fingers at the end of each arm. The fingers closely resembled talons with sharp claws. The feet of the creature were like large, flattened lumps without toes. The beast was male and naked with yellow skin that was covered in dirt or clay. It had "furrows" in its head, but the body was smooth. Along with Schmehl was another man named Jared Rissmiller, who had been helping him with the cattle drive. He corroborated Schmehl's tale and insisted that the beast had been startled by the cattle being driven by the gate. It stood up and darted toward Schmehl with its claws snapping and its arms or forelegs open as if to grab him. Then it had apparently changed its mind, turned, and fled into a cornfield nearby.

The men were understandably shaken and rattled by the beast. They secured the cattle and went to pursue it. They found it a second time lying in a ball near the fence on the other side of the cornfield. When it realized that it had been discovered again, it jumped up on two legs and blinked at them. Rissmiller described it: "It is yellowish brown in color, with no hair, small eyes and face, arms about fourteen inches long, legs somewhat longer, the hands and feet resembling those of a human being, and has two horns on the top of the head."

The two young men attempted to capture what became known as the "Yellow What-Is-It," but the beast eluded them and made a getaway into the woods beyond the fencerow.

Later, the young men's story was supported by that of another local resident named Mr. Heckman. Heckman encountered the beast only days later. He confirmed the description given by the others, but he offered up an explanation for the beast. He said that it had to be an escaped gorilla; however, no one had reported losing a gorilla, and the description does not seem to tally.

For the next several months, local folks reported strange encounters and odd footprints. Several farmers found strange tracks in the plowed fields after rainstorms. Others reported hearing strange cries in the woods at night. Some felt that something was following them along the darkened roads.

The disturbances got so bad that armed men with dogs went out at night to patrol the area and look for the beast. The What-Is-It was never captured.

Tommyknockers

Stephen King made the word "Tommyknockers" infamous in his novel about spaceships, aliens, and terror. Long before King spun his web of fear there were others who spoke the word in coal-mining regions of Pennsylvania. Tommyknockers were small spirits or sprites, akin to fairies and gnomes from the Old World. They were little creatures that cast a blue glow as they moved along. Tommyknockers were miners too. They stalked the dark, dank shafts of the mines and worked alongside the miners. At least they did if the miners treated them well.

Tommyknockers were often heard digging in the mines after the men had long stopped their work. They were industrious little fellows who influenced mine conditions and could lead miners to rich veins of coal ore.

Tommyknockers, however, were not pushovers. They required respect, too. Miners left pans of food, water, and even coins for the little blue sprites. It was believed that if the Tommyknockers did not get their pay from the men, that disasters would befall the mines.

Miners would tell of Tommyknockers who led rescuers to injured people, led men out of dirty dark shafts just seconds before collapses, and other deeds.

Although today people laugh at these old tales, some folks who live near mines still say they see the blue lights and hear the Tommyknockers digging away.

Big Cats

Despite the fact that the Pennsylvania Game Commission has insisted for many years that there are no mountain lions in Pennsylvania, stories of these and other big cats persist. Some stories can be dismissed as hoaxes or mistaken identities but other reports remain unexplained. Consider the following collection of strange big cat encounters and decide for yourself what is lurking in the wilderness.

A Cat Named Bertha

There are many strange things in the Black Forest of Pennsylvania's Tioga and Potter counties, not the least of which are the long-tailed big cats that have been reported from time to time. In his book, *Amazing Indeed*, folklorist Robert R. Lyman Sr. chronicled one such tale from September 1951 involving a man named Lynn Wycoff of Wharton, who earned part of his living as a trapper.

Wycoff set up fox traps throughout the area, but from time to time, other animals would get caught in them. Wycoff was checking his traps one day when he came across quite an oddity. In the trap was a large cat that looked very much like a bobcat, but it had a long tail. Bobcats have short stumpy tails.

Wycoff went back to his house and got a bear trap, and along with his father, he returned to the fox trap. Together the men managed to get the cat transferred to the larger trap. The beast had a terrible temper, and Wycoff was injured repeatedly while handling it.

Word spread quickly about the strange cat. Hundreds of people came to see it. It snarled and hissed and tried to attack the folks who got near the cage.

Wycoff named the cat Bertha, and she became a local wonder. Wycoff's father was quoted as saying that his son chose the name because he once knew a woman with a temper as foul as that of the cat.

Wycoff apparently took good care of the cat and it increased significantly in size. It grew much larger than the average bobcat. The cat's dark markings never changed, and it never showed any change in its disposition.

Apparently Bertha was not the first of her kind to be found in the Black Forest. More than one hundred years before, in 1840, a man named Burrel Lyman from Roulet reportedly killed two cats with similar markings and long tails.

The Camping Trip

Daniel's favorite memories of childhood were the camping trips that he and his grandfather used to take. They never went anywhere beyond the farmland that Pap owned, but that didn't matter. Usually they went down to the creek and put up a tent. Pap had a fire ring set up nearby and there they cooked hot dogs and baked beans and roasted marshmallows. They went swimming and hiking, and then they lay down in their hammocks and talked. Pap told Daniel stories of his childhood on that very same farm.

One night in late summer, when Daniel was about eleven years old, he and Pap were on one of their frequent summer camping trips. They had taken a four-wheeler down to the creek loaded with camping stuff and Pap's big white pup, named Snowball. They had set up the tent, gathered firewood, and cooked their dinner. It was a beautiful summer's evening, and they sat around the campfire feeding it dead wood long after darkness had finally arrived. The katydids were chirping a warning that frost was not far away, but no one was worrying about anything on that night.

It was nearly eleven o'clock when Pap finally said that it was time to pick up things and tidy up the camp until morning. As they stood to begin to bank the fire down and gather up any food scraps, a terrible scream came from a little island in the middle of the creek. Everyone froze. Even Snowball stopped chewing on his stick. Suddenly, the pup jumped up and darted for the tent.

Daniel looked at Pap with worried eyes. Pap motioned with his gnarled old hand for Daniel to stay still and silent. He slowly reached for his walking stick that lay nearby. Again the scream came from the little island. It was a cross between a baby crying and a woman screaming. It made the hair on Daniel's neck stand up. Then the smell reached them. It stunk like a tomcat spraying, only ten times stronger. At that moment, Pap motioned toward the four-wheeler. He then grabbed Snowball and ran for the four-wheeler. Daniel slid on the back and wrapped his arms tightly around his Pap's waist.

Suddenly, there was splashing from the creek as if something big was coming through the water toward them. Daniel heard one more scream, but he pressed his face into Pap's back and held on tighter than he ever had before. The machine lurched forward and shot up the little grassy path toward home. Daniel heard the splashing, but he never turned back.

Up at the house, Pap and Daniel pounded on the door. Daniel's mother was still up and she ran to the door to find two very frightened campers and one muddy dog tumbling into the house. The two talked over each other as they tried to relay the story.

Pap remembered that a week earlier he had been hiking alone near an old abandoned mill and had smelled that same strong stink from a tomcat. He had assumed then that a cat had sprayed there many times. Now he was not so sure. Perhaps it had been one very large cat spraying the area.

No one ever saw the cat that night, but Daniel and his pap always believed that they had run away from an attack by a mountain lion. Officially, Pennsylvania's mountain lion population has been extinct for half a century or more, but don't tell that to Daniel or his grandfather. They both believe that they encountered a mountain lion on their camping trip that night.

Backpackers See Strange Cat

There is nothing like the joy of summer to make folks want to get out and enjoy camping and hiking. For three friends in a little town along the Sinnemahoning Creek, the idea of a camping trip sounded like a great way to spend a sultry August weekend in 2003.

The three men decided that instead of backpacking in their provisions the whole way, they would drive the supplies up the trail as far as they could get them. Then they would go back and hike without so much weight to carry. They could then pick up the supplies along the way.

The men drove up the remote trail, dumped off the supplies, and turned back to park the truck at the trail mouth. They were making slow progress because of the steep, winding trail.

The driver suddenly saw a big cat running across the road in front of the truck. The others then saw it quite clearly in the late-morning sunlight. It had a long tail, thick legs, and was very dark in color. The cat sauntered off and jumped into the brush. The three men, though, were sure that they had seen a mountain lion cross their trail that day.

The Mountain Lion of Welsh Mountain

In 2007, residents of Salisbury Township in Lancaster County reported that they were seeing a large mountain lion on Welsh Mountain. Among the residents was Merv King, who told Susan Shapiro of WGAL News 8 that he had seen the big cat in the brushpiles near his home and also in the woods.

Members of the Stolzfus family also reported seeing the big cat in the woods of their rural property. One family member described it as "just sitting there looking at us, and he was the color of a darker colored lab." The big cat was standing near a brushpile, and with a flip of his long tail he ran away.

The official Pennsylvania Game Commission response was that there are no large cats left in Pennsylvania. Perhaps that is true, but the folks on Welsh Mountain are sure that they have been seeing something very real.

Big Cat Killed in Palo Alto

In the spring of 2004, people in the Palo Alto area of Schuylkill County reported seeing a large cat or mountain lion in the Stanford foothills area.

On May 17, 2004, a Palo Alto police officer saw the cat in a local neighborhood for the second time that day. The cat was seen by others within the proximity of schools, so the police made a decision to find the animal and kill it before it attacked any people. Several forces worked together to find the animal, conducting a property-by-property search. The cat was found in a tree at the front of the property at 1525 Walnut Drive. An officer shot and killed the big beast, and there was no doubt that it was a large, male mountain lion. The cat weighed in at 108 pounds. There was no indication of the origins of the beast, but the officer did kill a mountain lion.

Citizens of the surrounding area were not sure that this mountain lion was the same one that they had seen earlier. The one they saw appeared to have distinctive markings on it. It had attacked a horse and was seen in the proximity of several homes.

Mountain Lion in Wilkes-Barre

According to the *Wilkes-Barre Times Leader*, Chuck Litwin Jr. saw a large cat on September 16, 2006. It was 9:00 A.M. and Chuck had to stop his vehicle while the big cat ambled slowly across Route 92 in Wyoming County and then into a cornfield. It was only twenty feet in front of him.

Chuck, a hunter, was sure that what he saw was a mountain lion. He described it as a large, yellow cat about six feet long, with a long tail. It looked like any mountain lion that he had seen on television, he said.

The Black Cat in the Schoolyard

In the mid-1980s, there were two separate black cat sightings near the town of Hyndman in southern Bedford County. The first took place in the playground at the Hyndman Elementary School, which bordered the woods.

One spring day, the teachers let the smaller children out to play. The teacher on recess duty noticed that one little boy had strayed away from the main group of children, and she hurried to catch the child and turn him back from the woods. As she neared the child, she saw a large black cat slinking out of the woods, as if stalking the child. The beast was as big as a mountain lion and was moving low like any large cat did when it stalked prey. The teacher picked up the little boy and hurried back toward the building. Other teachers had seen the cat as well and hurried the children off the playground. The cat sighting was reported to the police and the story later appeared in the *Bedford County Shopper's Guide* newspaper.

The following week a little boy was in class daydreaming as he stared out the window. His teacher had been dealing with the children's spring fever for days, so she called the child to task for his lack of attention.

"Just what are you looking at?" she queried the child.

The little boy looked out the window and pointed. "I was watching the big cat out there."

The teacher turned in time to see a large black cat walking across the empty yard and into the woods. This account also made the local papers.

School was dismissed for the summer vacation only days later. In the fall, a new chain-link fence was built to keep the children from wandering off. There have been no more sightings of the black cat since that time.

Serpents

With the recent interest in cryptozoology, television shows have featured stories about gigantic snakes in Africa and South America and strange Stone Age lizards living in remote areas around the world. Pennsylvania has its fair share of stories about monster reptilian creatures. Reports of twenty-foot snakes slithering about have kept people's eyes open in the woods. Ghastly lizard creatures in the state's rivers and lakes have frightened more than a few people who go swimming, fishing, and boating in Pennsylvania's waters.

The Broad Top Snake

Perhaps the strangest reptilian creature in Pennsylvania is known as the Broad Top Snake. It has long been sighted in the mountains of Bedford and Fulton counties. The legend behind the Broad Top Snake is often repeated in folklore.

In the early 1920s, the village of Hopewell could be reached by a large old wooden bridge. It was rickety, but it had withstood many storms and floods. One year, a traveling circus planned to come to the area and sent advance men to scout out an area near Hopewell to set up their tents. The local town fathers wanted the circus to come to town, but they were worried about the heavy wagons crossing the old bridge. They asked that only one wagon at a time cross the bridge. It really sounded like a simple request and the circus owner willingly agreed, but when he realized how slowly the circus would have to cross the bridge to do it that way, he ordered things to speed up. This meant that instead of one wagon being on the bridge at a time, up to three wagons could be on the bridge at a given time.

At first the bridge held as the wagons came rumbling across, but then the bridge groaned and snapped. A major support post gave way and the bridge fell more than twenty feet into the Juniata River. The wagons full of animals for the circus went down, too. The big cat wagon and the reptile wagons crashed into the rock-strewn river. Many of the animals escaped.

According to the story, at least one large boa constrictor was never recovered, although some versions say it was an anaconda. It was several years, however, before folks up on the Broad Top had reason to recall the story of the circus wagon and the lost snake. It was then that people began to report that they had seen a giant snake on the Broad Top. It was long enough to cross the entire two-lane highway and thicker in girth than a telephone pole. The snake moved slowly without any fear of being seen. Folks on the Broad Top concluded that the snake was the mutant spawn of the escaped boa constrictor and a black snake with which it had mated in the old coal mines there. They believed that in the winters, the hybrid snake hid in the mines, living off rats it consumed.

Among the older stories is one about an elderly couple who were crossing Broad Top Mountain when they had to swerve to miss what they took to be a tree in the road. They missed the downed tree, but struck a standing one. As the elderly couple sat in the car discussing what had just happened and how they were going to get help on the lonely road, one of them suddenly saw the fallen tree begin to move. In horror, they watched as the tree lifted its head and they realized that what they were witnessing wasn't really a tree but a snake—a giant snake. They later told a police officer that the snake looked like a log and was long enough that it spanned both sides of the road.

In the late 1980s, a woman named Paula, who had grown up on the Broad Top, described her experience with the giant snake. "I know that you don't think that the Broad Top snake is real," she began her story, "but I know that it is.

"It all began about ten years ago. My dad and mom live up on the Broad Top on an old farm. Each year my dad invites the whole family to go hunting up there with him. My husband and I always go. That year buck season came in cold and wet, but there was no snow. Now any hunter will tell you that that's the most miserable weather they could have to hunt in. You want snow to track the deer in. The rain is just cold and miserable.

"Anyhow, my dad had a deer stand up in a tree and he settled up there. I followed my husband further up the mountain. Frankly, Dad's days of running up the mountain were nearly done. He just wasn't up to it, so the deer stand gave him a good way to hunt.

"We all were listening for the other one to get off a shot, but all day long there was nothing. It was like someone had told the deer to go hide. We didn't see a rack all day long. Finally, about dusk, we started back. What we didn't know was that Dad had seen something else just before dusk.

"Dad had been sitting up in his stand late in the afternoon, looking around for a set of deer horns, when he first saw the movement. It was almost surreal to watch the big snake coming down through the field. The snake was horribly large.

"Dad would later estimate that it was twenty feet long. He watched as the snake approached his deer stand. He was really shaking. He gathered the gun and waited for the snake to attack him.

"None of us knew it, and so we just walked back to the farmhouse and waited for Dad. When he didn't come at dark, my husband and I could see the worry on my mom's face, and we decided to take a walk out to the stand and see what was going on. I was beginning to get pretty worried myself. Dad was a stickler for paying attention to the laws, and you can't hunt at night legally. My husband tried to cheer us up by saying that Dad had probably fallen asleep or something.

"When we got to the deer stand we called out for him, and then my husband climbed up. Dad was sitting up there sort of crouched over, clutching his gun and he was pale. He looked like he was having a heart attack and he was. We got him back to the house and got help. Dad thankfully survived the heart attack, and he would later tell us about seeing the snake. It was his fear of the snake that brought on the heart attack.

"Even then I might not have believed in the snake if not for the fact that two years later my husband and I saw it while we were hunting. It was the biggest thing I had ever seen. I thought it could swallow a human being. I know it could have swallowed a child."

Paula's story is strange, but then there's the story of a businessman in Altoona. He said that as a teenager he lived in Johnstown and on weekends he and his father would pack up their dirt bikes and go to the Broad Top to ride through the old abandoned strip mine areas. One day, they were riding along when what looked like a large fallen tree made them stop. As the father and son looked at the tree and discussed the options, one end of the tree popped up in the air and they saw a large snake's head. The snake began to undulate, and then it moved off. The man said that the snake carried its head off the ground like a cobra does. That ended the dirt bike rides on the Broad Top for them.

In the 1990s, the snake made the newspapers once more when it was sighted by three local men. According to one man's interview, the three men had been riding to a construction job every morning. All summer long they had made it a point to stop at a spring on the Broad Top to fill their watercooler with good springwater for the day. One morning, the men were filling the cooler when they saw the giant snake. It slithered past them and away from them, but they got a good look at it. Their description of the size and color were consistent with the previous reports.

Lizard in a Drain

The air was cold in the New Kensington area northeast of Pittsburgh on a raw March day in 1981, but the children in the playground were not overly troubled by it. They wore warm mittens, boots, hats, and thick coats. Several boys were playing near a large drainage pipe, when they saw a small lizardlike creature about three feet tall walking on two feet out of the pipe. The children froze as they watched the beast for a second. They picked up sticks and rocks and quickly began to give chase to the beast. The shouts of the children alerted some nearby adults who also saw it. The little creature cried out when pelted and took off running. It ran through the park back toward the drainage pipe and quickly darted back inside.

The children and adults who saw the beast agreed that it looked like a cross between a human and a lizard. They later said that they got the impression that the creature was not an adult, but they couldn't say why. The lizard was never seen again.

Lake Erie's Sea Monster

Long before the first European ever set sail on what is now called Lake Erie, the local Indians knew of a strange creature that could cause them harm. They tried to warn the settlers about the beast that plied the waters and stalked the shores of the great lake, but the settlers would not believe them—at least not until they began to have their own experiences.

Stories of the creature were whispered along the shore towns for many years and nearly forgotten at times, but it was not until the 1930s that the old tales were resurrected. At that time, a carnival barker and his partner created a sensation when they claimed that they had captured the beast while out fishing and had brought it back to town. The story caught the attention of a New York reporter who was vacationing on the lake. The reporter did a fantastic job of publicizing the story, but it was eventually considered to be a hoax, and a lot of very angry folks were left feeling duped.

After that scam, it took fifty years before the creature again was taken seriously. Starting in the early 1980s, the beast seemed to make several appearances and had now garnered a name—Bessie. Bessie is not exactly a friendly creature, however. A young woman named Brenda McCormack claimed to have encountered the creature while paddling the lake and she had a terrible story to tell.

Brenda was swimming and paddling along one summer evening when something bit the young woman on the leg. The girl pulled free and managed to make it to shore. She had a bite on her legs with teeth marks six inches apart. She believed it to be the work of Bessie. Skeptics offered up the theory that

Brenda had been attacked by a bowfish. Others speculated that the aggressive fish was a lake sturgeon. These fish can weigh over 300 pounds and are up to fourteen feet long. Throughout that summer, on the other side of Lake Erie in Port Dover, Ontario, several other people were bitten by a strange lake creature, too.

Throughout the years, there have been other people who have claimed to see the beast, mostly boaters and sailors. Bessie has been described as a horse-headed creature with a long body like an eel. Others say that they have seen the humps of the creature as she floated through the waters.

There have even been a few reports of people seeing the beast on land. Those who have seen her on the shore claim that she has short, squat legs and a grey-green long body.

Ogua

The idea of a large river monster in the Ohio and Mononga-hela rivers near Pittsburgh might sound funny, but such a creature is said to exist. This beast is called Ogua and was known to the natives of western Pennsylvania before the first Europeans came to the area.

The natives warned the settlers that Ogua was large and serpentine with snapping jaws capable of biting into a man and carrying him to a watery death. It was believed that Ogua dragged its prey underwater, where it held it until it drowned.

Although Ogua was mostly a creature of the water, it was capable of wandering on land, too. It was said to venture away from the rivers on stout, squat legs, and it moved very fast for short periods of time. There are old accounts of strange disappearances along the rivers, but very little else is known about this elusive water monster.

The Death of Maggie May

It was a warm summer's day in Acosta, Somerset County, in 1939, and young Helen Koke was lounging around with her sister and their girlfriends. Helen was only twelve years old that summer, but she was already a responsible young woman. She was doing most of the housework for her invalid mother and part of the cooking. This day was a rare treat for young Helen, for it was a lazy day when the girls could take a walk, swim, or simply lay and watch the clouds roll by while they chatted about their future lives.

At some point that afternoon, Helen and the other girls decided that a cool dip in the local creek was in order, and they took off without a care in the world. Their bare feet slapped the dusty dirt road and they alternated between running and a loafing walk.

As they passed by a stretch of woods at the foot of a large hill, the girls paused because they thought that they might have heard something. They then heard the raspy sound again and began to look around. It only took a moment to locate the source of the sound. It was coming from behind a clump of bushes. When the girls stepped behind the bushes, they were shocked and horrified.

On the ground was an elderly local woman named Maggie May. She was a rather rotund little woman with frumpy old clothes and tousled hair. The girls found the old woman gasping for air for a terrible reason. A large black snake had wrapped itself around her chest and was literally squeezing the life out of her.

The girls were terrified to get close, but they were now able to hear the old woman's words. Maggie begged them to go for help and the girls turned to run. Helen stayed with her. While the other girls ran for help, Helen tried to think of anything that she could do to help the old woman, but the snake was too big. Maggie told her that she had sat down against a tree to rest and had awakened because she was having difficulty breathing. It was then that she saw the snake. Her frantic attempts to dislodge the beast had only made the snake more determined to squeeze her chest.

By the time help arrived, Maggie was no longer able to make a sound. She had lost consciousness. Helen could not help thinking that it was a blessing, for the men had to beat the snake to death and cut it in pieces to get it off of her. It was estimated that the snake was four to five inches wide and about fifteen feet long. Maggie never recovered from her ordeal and died shortly thereafter. For the rest of her life, Helen remembered the sad story of the day that a monster snake killed Maggie May.

Creatures of the Air

The idea of giant birds flapping their way through the state might sound silly, but Pennsylvania has been home to such creatures for more than two hundred years. Thunderbirds are far from the mythical creatures of western American lore. They have been spotted in Pennsylvania's skies, along with none other than the Jersey Devil, who glides across the border from time to time.

The Jersey Devil

Today there is no way to know exactly how the legend of the Jersey Devil first began. The most common version of the story is that in 1735 there was a woman living in New Jersey's Pine Barrens named Mother Leeds who had twelve children. She could barely keep the family clothed and fed as it was, but then matters got worse when she discovered that she was with child yet again. Thirteen children, Mother Leeds shuddered. She cried out over her anger of having yet another mouth to feed. "May the Devil take this child," she cursed. When the child was born, the Devil indeed did take it. Within moments of the child's birth, it began to mutate. The feet turned to hooves, the head became that of a horse, and the body grew larger. Leathery wings sprouted from its back and a forked tail emerged below. The newborn beast attacked its mother and killed the midwife before escaping into a wild and stormy night.

Thus goes a popular version of the tale. But stories were told about a creature that stalked the Pine Barrens long before Mother Leeds learned of her ill-fated thirteenth child. The Swedes who settled there before the English called the area "Drake Kill," which translates into "Dragon Kill." Long before that the Lenape called the area "Popuessing," or "Place of the Dragon." Whatever the origins of this creature, it doesn't seem to recognize state lines. It has wandered over the border into Pennsylvania on numerous occasions.

In January 1909 the creature left footprints throughout the region of Bristol, Pennsylvania. Some said it was a hoax, but if it was, the prankster was very dedicated. The hoofprints went through yards, on rooftops, over fences, and across fields and woods. There were no human prints noticed near the hoofprints.

On the night of January 16, several people in Bristol reported seeing the beast flying over the town. A police officer later reported that it was a large winged beast that made a terrible screeching noise. On that same night another resident of Bristol claimed to see the Jersey Devil. He described it as "having a ram-like head with curled horns, a long neck, thin wings, and four legs, the front pair shorter than the back." The following morning, miles of hoofprints were found in the snow and attributed to the Jersey Devil.

On January 18, postmaster E. W. Minster of Bristol was awakened at 2:00 A.M. by a haunting sound from the Delaware River. It was such a strange sound that it compelled him to get up and check it out. He looked out his window and saw a strange creature like a "large crane" flying across the night sky, glowing softly. The beast had thin wings, long back legs, short front legs, and a long neck. The cry it emitted was somewhere between a whistle and a squeal. In sheer shock, Minster watched the beast as it faded into the darkness.

Not far from Bristol on the following night, a Mr. and Mrs. Evans awoke to the sound of a large animal tromping on their shed roof. They looked outside and saw a beast "about three-and-a-half feet high, with a face like a collie and a head like a horse. It had a long neck, wings about two feet long—and its back legs were like those of a crane and it had horse's hooves. It walked on its back legs and held up two short front legs with paws on them."

Over the following days, the beast wreaked havoc on the area. It chased a Mrs. White out of her yard. She said that the beast breathed flames at her. She screamed and ran for her home. Her husband hurried to the door in time to see his wife running toward the house with a beast giving chase and spitting flames behind her.

Back in New Jersey, a Mrs. Sorbinski heard her dog yelping in pain and hurried outside to find the Devil attacking the canine. She grabbed a broom and beat the beast until it let go of her pet. The beast bit off a bit of the dog before fleeing. Mrs. Sorbinski pulled her wounded dog inside and alerted the authorities. The police arrived at the house and found a large crowd gathered outside. Some of the people claimed to have heard terrible cries coming from the darkness, but no one else sighted the Devil.

Devil hunts, with rewards of up to $10,000, suddenly became the rage. Vigilante groups stalked both Pennsylvania and New Jersey looking for the beast. But the Jersey Devil slipped away to hide once more. The now defunct *Philadelphia Record* reported many of the Jersey Devil's exploits. The coverage became so extensive that the stories were picked up nationally.

Every night for that entire week people spotted the Jersey Devil, heard its terrible cries, or saw the footprints. The stories were reported by businessmen, government officials, police officers, and citizens of upright standing.

Soon, word was sent out that the beast had been cornered in a barn in Morrisville, Pennsylvania. The authorities investigated and were shocked to find that the beast had escaped. That night a police officer from Woodbury, New Jersey, saw the Devil flying over his town. Shortly after, the beast was spotted in Salem, Pennsylvania, where more than one hundred people saw it.

As quickly as the Jersey Devil came on the scene, it left once more. No one reported any more sightings until 1927, when a cab driver was changing a tire one evening near the town of Salem. He had finished the tire change and was putting away his tools when the car suddenly began to shake. He looked up to see a huge, winged creature pounding on the car roof. The man dove into the car, leaving behind the rest of his tools. He took off and went to the Salem police to report the sighting.

In 1930, the creature returned to Leeds Point, New Jersey, where it was seen feeding on berries in the Barrens near Mays Landing. The beast was seen feeding in the area on other occasions.

The beast has been seen many times since then. In the 1960s, the local police began to post signs saying that the Jersey Devil was all a hoax. Still, sightings of the beast continued, and continue to this day.

In more recent years, a resident of Howell Township, Pennsylvania, saw a creature similar to the Jersey Devil several times between 1968 and 1970. He even reported that he shot at the creature, but the bullet did not affect it.

In 1970, a woman in Mercer County told authorities that a large creature flew over her yard and picked up her little girl. She blamed the beast for pulling hair out of her child's head.

The Jersey Devil has been seen elsewhere, from Canada to Texas, and is frequently reported in New Jersey, Pennsylvania, and New York. It has variously been described as having ram's horns, and either a dog's head or a horse's head. It is described as from three to five feet tall, with colors that range from white to black. The beast has been observed eating berries, but has been associated with livestock deaths, particularly chicken and geese. The creature has been shot at on multiple occasions and was once seen tangled in a power line. A body was once found that was presumed to be that of the Devil.

A Cemetery Flyover

In 2001, Pastor Robin Swope took a position at a local cemetery in Erie County as a groundskeeper and gravedigger to help fund a new organization he had started. It was a good job that allowed him to work in peaceful surroundings and to be outside.

One hot day in July, Robin was given the assignment to mow the twenty-three acres of property from the mausoleum to the area of high-tension powerlines. He set off on his mower intent on completing his task. As he got to the area, the sound of the riding mower seemed to startle something in the bushes about twenty-five yards away from him. To Robin's surprise, a very large bird flew from the bushes and struggled to take flight. The bird launched itself upward and began to soar past a series of high-tension wires. Judging by the power pylons, Robin was able to estimate that the bird's wingspan was very large—larger than any bird he had ever seen.

The bird drifted off above the trees and disappeared into the sky. For a moment, Robin sat on the mower and simply stared after the creature. He had been hearing about Thunderbirds ever since he was a child, but he had never seriously expected to see one. Suddenly, he jumped off the mower and began to shout, "Yes! Yes! Yes!" in his excitement.

Later Robin described the bird as "both similar to many large birds that I had seen in the area and yet very distinct. It looked downright primitive. It had no neck, a thin and very pointed beak, and a long tail that ended in what looked to be a triangle. It was completely black or dark gray from the head to the tail with no visible markings on it except a small bulge of plumage under the neck that stuck close to the body. . . . I estimated the wingspan of the creature to be anywhere from fifteen to seventeen feet in length."

Robin later asked around and found that he alone saw the strange bird. He was still not exactly sure what he saw and thought of his experience as "a possible Thunderbird sighting." He did send a letter about his sighting to *Fortean Times*, which published it in the August 2001 edition.

Later, Robin learned that paranormal researcher Stan Gordon had received a report of another Thunderbird sighting from a party only fifty miles away in Greensburg. That person stated that he saw a large bird "the size of a small airplane" from his living room window. The report said that the witness described the bird as "dark brown or black . . . the body was not bulky and the overall appearance was not like any bird he had ever seen." The bird settled in a tree approximately three hundred yards from the witness's house and stayed there for nearly twenty minutes. It was coming from the north and headed south. At first, the witness had mistaken the shadow for that of the ultralight aircraft that his neighbors flew. He had looked out the window expecting to see it gliding in, but saw the bird instead. He later estimated that the creature's body was approximately five feet long and its wingspan was about fifteen feet.

Years went by and Robin moved on from his job at the cemetery, but he never quite let go of his sighting of the bird.

In April 2009, he was with a paranormal investigative team that was planning to do an investigation in the same cemetery where he had once worked. It was near sunset and he decided to get a few photographs of the high-tension wires where he had seen the bird in 2001 for an article he was preparing about his sighting. He snapped his photos and then stowed the camera in the car. He turned to walk toward the mausoleum when he heard noises in the brush to his north.

He turned and ran back to retrieve the camera. A large bird rose up out of the brush and made gliding circles as it gained altitude. Smaller birds seemed to be pestering it. Robin recognized it as the same type of bird he had seen years earlier. He struggled to get the camera up and capture some shots, but between the speed of the bird and battery problems, he managed only one shot. The photograph is of a large bird between the power pylons. The bird is a bit indistinct, because of movement, but does appear to be very large. It was black, but was missing the white tuff Robin had seen on the first bird. Like the first bird, its wingspan was about fifteen feet. Robin later said that both birds resembled a great blue heron in shape, but were at least twice as large and had a slightly different shape.

Carried Off by a Thunderbird?

In August 1897 on a sultry summer evening, a nineteen-year-old farmhand named Thomas Eggleton walked to the town of Hammersley Fork in Clinton County to mail a letter to his mother. Eggleton was always a good employee who never got himself into trouble, so his employer thought nothing of his evening outing.

By the next morning, Eggleton still had not returned to the farm. His employer began to worry. It was not like Tom to be out all night. The employer began walking to town, tracing

Eggleton's footprints in the soft dirt. He lost them near the town, but later bloodhounds picked them up and followed them to the middle of the bridge, where the scent apparently stopped. What could have happened to make the boy's scent stop in the middle of a bridge? People started a search and they dragged the river, but Eggleton's body was not found.

Local folks began to mutter that a Thunderbird had carried off the young man. Some people claimed to have seen a massive bird just prior to Eggleton's disappearance. Caution spread throughout the area, and schools actually closed for two weeks.

Four years later, word from Eggleton arrived. His former employer received a letter from him explaining that he had recently awakened in a hospital in South Africa and had remembered that he had worked for a farmer outside of Hammersley Fork. Eggleton could shed no light on how he came to be in South Africa, and he had no memory of any of his past. Theories about Eggleton's disappearance abound. Some people believe that he slipped through the fabric of time. Others believe that he was abducted by a Thunderbird.

Close Encounters of the Bird Kind

In 1937, in the Black Forest region, a four-year-old girl was out picking berries in the countryside with her family when she gave out a terrified scream. The family was shocked to see a large black bird in the sky. The bird was blamed for the girl's subsequent disappearance.

Only four years later, Barney Pluff, a seventy-four-year-old man, went missing. It happened at the same time that others were reporting Thunderbird sightings. The local belief was that one of the birds had attacked and eaten or killed and carried off the frail old man.

In the summer of 1969, Albert Schoonover paused along a rural road near Kettle Creek Lake in Potter County when he and two highway workers watched a large black bird swoop over the lake. The bird was massive and it dove toward the ground and came up with a live fawn. They estimated that the fawn weighed at least fifteen pounds.

In the Robbins Run area during the early 1970s, a Lock Haven couple was surprised by a large, dive-bombing black bird that seemed to be headed straight for their car. At the last second they saw it touch down on the road and grab up a dead groundhog. The bird timed the maneuver so close that it barely missed the couple. The woman had a close view of the bird's talon and later said that it was four times the size of her own hand. On June 8, 1971, Linda Edwards and a passenger were driving along a road near Jersey Shore when they came upon a Thunderbird eating a dead opossum on the road. Linda estimated that the bird's wingspan as it took off was approximately eighteen feet wide.

In August 1973, two women were traveling near the Ole Bull Museum at Carter Camp on their way home one night. They were driving along in their Volkswagen when they rounded a turn at Sunderlinville. Suddenly, a large bird took flight on their left side. It startled the women because its wingspan was large enough to nearly cross the entire two-lane road. The bird struck the side of the vehicle and one woman later said, "It flew against the side of the vehicle, swiped at the front end, and tried to attack us." The younger woman gunned the engine and sped away. The other woman was sure the bird would have killed them if it had been able to reach them.

The Capture of a Thunderbird

The following story about the capture of a Thunderbird comes from *Amazing Indeed* by Robert R. Lyman Sr.

In 1898, a Crawford County farmer near the town of Centerville noticed that one of his cows was dead in his field. He dragged the animal off to the edge of a field where he could later bury it. After a few days, the farmer noticed a large black creature out by the dead cow. He knew that whatever it was, it meant no good for his animals. The farmer decided that before he buried the dead cow, he would use it as bait and set a trap to catch the predator. To the farmer's shock, the creature he found in the trap was beyond his imagination. He had trapped a huge bird that he could not identify.

The farmer decided to take the beast home rather than kill it. At home, he placed it in a large cage. Over the next few days, he began to ask around about what type of bird he had captured.

The superintendent of Potter County schools, A. P. Akeley, later described the bird as approximately five feet tall, with a short neck and short legs. It was gray in color. The superintendent said he did not believe that the bird was a vulture, because the colors, size, and shape did not match the species.

Attack of the Thunderbird

In 1973, Wanda and Joseph Kaye were driving along a road in the area known as the Black Forest, when their eyes caught something moving at the side of the road ahead of them. Wanda turned toward the motion and realized that she was seeing a huge bird. The bird was flapping its wings and running toward the car. Wanda cried out, drawing her husband's attention toward the charging bird. It had a huge wingspan and Wanda thought that the giant bird was about to attack the car.

Inside the car, Wanda was able to see that the bird had white feathers on its legs and head and its body was black. Wanda was sure that the bird was not going to be able to take off in time to avoid crashing into their vehicle, but at the last second the draft caused by the vehicle speeding forward caught under the bird's wings and it touched the window of the car as it soared upward.

Later researchers postulated that the bird had not meant to attack the car at all, but rather was using the lift of the wind from the car to help get it off the ground. There have been many reports of Thunderbirds that appeared to have difficulty getting airborne at first.

Incident at Cross Fork Creek

October 14, 1973, was a bright cool fall day in the Black Forest region of Pennsylvania. Bob Lyman and his family were at their camp at Cross Fork Creek. He had invited several friends to visit them for the day. While he and his wife Mary Ellen, his mother, and six others were unloading supplies, they noticed something large flying above them that blocked out the sun briefly. They looked up and saw three large birds with approximately fifteen-foot wingspans flying overhead. Bob was well aware of what he was seeing, because his father was Robert Lyman Jr., who had chronicled several stories of Thunderbirds in his books.

Bob was fifty-two years old at the time, and his family had been going to the camp for many years and had never seen such a creature. He and his companions were very excited by the sighting. Only about twenty minutes later, nine more guests arrived. They listened in fascination to the account. Two of the younger members of the group decided that the birds might still be in the area. They agreed to take radios and climb the hills nearby to see if they could get a glimpse of the giant birds.

The men grabbed radios and headed for the outcroppings above the camp. They looked around for some time before one of the men got on his radio and reported that he saw a large bird flying down the valley toward the camp. The outcropping gave the young fellow a great observation point. The bird flew by at approximately the same level. The young man later reported that the bird was gray in color and had a wingspan of approximately fifteen feet. It was a rare opportunity to observe the Thunderbird in action. One of the things that the observer commented on was the languid flapping of the large bird's wings.

Everyone at the camp that weekend observed at least one of the three birds, and all fifteen of them agreed that, as far as they knew, the birds were of an unknown species.

Werewolves

Pennsylvania might seem like an odd place to encounter werewolves, but there have long been tales of wolfmen or dogmen stalking the environs of the state. The tales of werewolves came to America with the German immigrants who settled vast sections of Pennsylvania. Although there are few reports of encounters in the state, the stories span back into the eighteenth century and continue today.

Protected by a Werewolf

May Paul was a young farmgirl in Northumberland County in the late nineteenth century. One of May's main jobs was watching the flock of sheep that provided wool that helped the family earn a living. May spent her days walking the fields looking for the best grazing area for her sheep. It was during this time that May made the acquaintance of an old man from the area.

The old man was known in the area to be a hermit. He never associated with anyone, and he really didn't associate with May either. But he did keep her company in his own way. He often came and sat at the edge of the fields to watch the young woman tend her flocks. He always showed great respect, and so May began to draw out the old man. He began to talk to her for a bit and they eventually became friends.

Unfortunately, local gossip wasn't as kind to the old fellow. No one knew anything about him, not even his name, and folks were suspicious of him. People wondered how he made a living, where he lived, and exactly who he was.

At about the same time that the old fellow had appeared, wolves began to attack livestock in the local area. People muttered how strange it was to suddenly have so many wolf attacks. Someone thought that there might be a connection between the strange man and the wolves.

The old people remembered the stories of werewolves and wondered if this man could be one. They knew that werewolves commanded natural wolves, and they noticed that May Paul's flock of sheep was the only one in the area that did not suffer losses because of attacks.

May's parents cautioned her against befriending the old man, but May saw no harm in her kindness to him. She continued their quiet friendship despite the local gossip. She also noticed something strange, however, about the old man and the wolves. Several times she had seen packs of wolves circling her sheep. She would try to fend them off, but then suddenly the wolves would slink away as if frightened by something. May began to realize that each time this had happened the old man had appeared as if he had been watching over her.

The wolf attacks continued for several years despite wolf hunts. During that time, May continued her friendship with the old man and her sheep remained safe.

One night, an old farmer heard a commotion in his barn and hurried out with a gun to see what was happening. He stopped short in the barnyard when a grizzled old wolf came running past him. The farmer raised his gun and shot at the wolf, wounding it. The wolf ran off and the farmer pursued it for a short distance. The farmer then realized that it was not wise to be hunting for a wounded wolf in the darkness and decided to return home. He would track the wolf in the daylight.

The next morning, the farmer did track the wolf to a thicket of bushes. He pushed aside the brush and found the body of the old man who had befriended May. The old man had died from loss of blood from a gunshot wound in his chest.

The story quickly circulated about the wolf, the old man, and the farmer. May was terribly sad to hear that her friend had suffered such a violent death. She maintained staunchly that the stories were wicked and cruel. The old man had been a kind person and not a werewolf.

But there are those who would disagree. The wolf attacks seemed to stop shortly after the old man's death. The old man's ghost was even seen sitting on a log in the field where May tended her sheep. At other times, a grizzled old gray wolf was seen turning back wolves about to attack May's sheep. People said that the werewolf was protecting May—even from the dead. Today, the area where the old man was shot is called "Die Woolf Man's Grob" in memory of the event.

The Bloodsucking Beast

Farmers work hard to build safe shelters to protect their livestock from predators. But for farmers in the Erie area in 1891, their best efforts did little to protect their animals. According to newspaper accounts, the poultry farmers of that region were fighting a desperate battle that summer.

During the night, several farmers and other locals reported seeing a fur-covered, humanoid beast that walked on two feet. This creature was credited with having killed more than six hundred chickens, geese, and ducks throughout the summer.

The poor fowl had their heads ripped off. The beast then sucked the blood from their necks until it could get no more. Then it cast the bodies to the ground.

The farmers were unable to stop the beast. It got through fences, tore open cages, and ripped apart coops. The farmers were both angry and upset about the livestock losses, but they were unable to catch or kill the beast. Eventually, the beast left the area, because the poultry deaths stopped.

Whispers from Western Pennsylvania

Today, the idea of werewolves might seem farfetched, but there are still strange little tales that reach out from the wilderness of the Pennsylvania-Ohio border. On several occasions, Bigfoot researchers from the area have heard strange murmurings about such things. A man who will be called Hank tells a story that is nothing short of amazing.

Hank frequented a store not far from the border that carried organic items and holistic medicines. He was surprised one day to find a Going Out of Business sign in the window of the store. Hank decided to go in and check out the bargains.

When he entered, he found the woman who ran the shop pulling down a display. He had spoken to her several times before, so he asked her why she was shutting down. Hank always thought that the store did a good business and she affirmed that it had done well enough. Hank asked her again, "Why are you closing down?"

The woman looked nearly frightened by his innocent question. Finally, she walked over and checked the door to be sure that no one was near it. "I probably shouldn't say anything," she said, walking back closer to Hank. "But I'm terribly frightened and I just have to tell someone. If I remember correctly, you're a ghost hunter, so maybe you won't think that I'm totally crazy."

Hank affirmed that he wouldn't think that the shopkeeper was crazy and then promised to keep her secret until she was gone.

"About a month ago," the shopkeeper began, "a man came in here and asked me for some herbs. He also wanted belladonna, and I explained to him that it was a hallucinogen and that it's prohibited to sell it. He then asked for some other herbs and wolf's bane. I laughed and said, 'Are you planning to become a werewolf or what?' because I recognized the herbs as having once been used in concoctions for that long ago.

"I couldn't believe the change that came over the man. He grabbed my wrist and squeezed it until it really hurt. 'Why do you say that?' he demanded.

"I laughed to calm him down and told him that it was just a joke. The man looked angry, almost evil. He threatened me. 'I belong to a group of werewolves that meet in one of the state parks. We hunt and mate and are free there. We need the herbs. You'll get them for us.' He was really frightening me now. I don't know if what he said was true or not, but I know that he believed what he said.

"Well I sold him the herbs and was glad to be rid of him. He's come back once since then to reinforce his threats to kill me if I talked. He claims that he and his fellow werewolves were responsible for a dog attack that made the paper a couple weeks ago. Anyhow, I don't care if he's for real or not. I just think that he's scary. I'm selling out and moving. I know that it sounds crazy, but I half believe the fellow. You didn't see his eyes when he talked to me. There is something wrong with him. I'm not even going to open a shop where I move to. I don't want him to ever find me again."

The woman shuddered and glanced around. She smiled as if to soften the strange story. "Anyhow I'm leaving. Just please don't say anything until I leave next week. I'm afraid of him."

Hank promised not to talk and he never mentioned it for over a year. He couldn't resist asking me if I had ever heard of such a thing. I must have looked a bit surprised, for only months earlier, a friend of mine who collects Bigfoot tales had encountered a very frightened young man just over the border in Ohio who claimed to have encountered a werewolf very near the park that the woman had spoken of.

A Werewolf at College

Two college students who will be called Jess and Parker were juniors at West Chester University. One Friday evening, the young men decided to go barhopping with their friends. As the night progressed, they went from establishment to establishment, and at each stop they drank. Although the young men were feeling no pain, they did not consider themselves to be drunk. As the evening wore on, they decided that they would continue their drinking elsewhere.

The young students stopped and picked up a couple six packs before walking over to Everhart Park, a peaceful part of town. They had been to the park many times before and knew its layout well. There is a main path lined with trees and there are lights along the path. The young men decided that they would go back the path where they could not be seen before they began to drink.

Jess and Parker sat down in the grass about halfway down the path and opened a beer. They were just talking and enjoying the beautiful evening when they noticed something at the end of the path. Both students paused to watch the figure moving in the shadows. "What is that?" Parker hissed. The two could barely make out the figure moving in the shadows where the light did not penetrate. They watched the figure for a few seconds more, before deciding it must be a tramp.

Jess and Parker were admittedly drunk enough by now that they thought about hassling the tramp, but while they discussed it, the figure stepped back into the shadows and disappeared. For about ten minutes they waited and watched as they tried to decide where the tramp had gone, but at last the lure of the alcohol called them back and they began to chat and drink once more.

For nearly an hour, the two boys sat talking as they drank. By now some of the worst of the buzz was wearing off and Jess began to feel a bit uncomfortable. He glanced up repeatedly, as if expecting to see someone watching them. The skin on the back of his neck began to crawl. He was sure that there was someone in the darkness listening and watching them. His first thought was that the tramp had returned. He leaned forward to whisper his suspicion to Parker. Parker glanced around looking for a shadow that moved.

Suddenly, a large wolflike creature threw itself forward out of the bushes and lunged at the boys. For one dazzling second, the young men struggled to comprehend what they were seeing. Although the creature had the head of a wolf, its body was like that of a man. The creature stood on two legs, not four. It bared its teeth and growled as any wolf would do. The young men jumped up leaving behind their beer and took off running. They turned and headed toward the campus as fast as they could go.

Jess and Parker might never have mentioned their strange encounter again had it not been for one further event. One night they were goofing off with a bunch of friends when they decided to confide the story to them. Both young men knew that they'd probably get laughed out of the place, but it was just too good a story keep to themselves. To their surprise, one of their friends looked at them seriously and told them that they weren't the only ones to have reported seeing strange creatures around West Chester. It turned out that there had been other stories of a wolflike creature in the area.

Kelly was a freshman. She pulled into the parking lot at Farrell Stadium. There was no game that night, so Kelly agreed to pick up her girlfriend Leslie there when she finished studying at the library. Kelly was still learning about the West Chester area that fall, so the stadium was an easy and convenient spot to meet.

Kelly pulled her car to a stop and put it in park while letting the engine idle. She was surprised that Leslie was not already there waiting for her. It was 11:00 P.M. and the two girls had agreed to meet at 10:30 P.M., but Kelly had gotten twisted around in the unfamiliar town. She fully expected Leslie would be ready to lecture her for letting her stand alone in the dark.

Kelly watched anxiously out of her car windows as she waited for some shadow to move. She began to wonder if everything was okay with Leslie. She picked up her cell phone and dialed Leslie's phone. It rang but Leslie didn't pick up. Kelly looked out at the empty lot. She began to feel as if she were not alone.

Kelly had pulled in so that she was facing the field, and it was there that she first saw movement. The darkness began to sway and twist as it moved toward her, and she realized that someone was running in her direction. Suddenly, all sorts of uncomfortable thoughts filled her mind. Was that Leslie running? If so, what was she running from? Had someone found her alone and tried to harm her? Kelly sat up anxiously, waiting to make out the figure in the dark. She slid the gear shifter to drive and placed her foot on the brake. She was ready in case it was not Leslie.

Leslie burst across the parking lot, clawed for the car door, opened it, and threw herself inside. "Go," she screamed. "Get us out of here now!"

Kelly placed her foot firmly on the gas and turned around in the empty lot.

Beside her, Leslie gasped for air. She was winded by her run.

"What's going on?" Kelly demanded, glancing at her friend. "What are you running from? What was out there?"

Leslie pulled a ragged breath. "A wolf!" Leslie gasped. "I was being chased by a wolf!"

Kelly could not help looking at her friend suspiciously. "There are no wolves in West Chester," she said. Leslie's breathing was evening out. "Well maybe it wasn't a wolf," she allowed. "It was something strange. I thought it ran on two legs part of the time."

Now Kelly was sure that either Leslie was joking or someone was playing a joke on her. A wolf that ran on two legs part of the time had to be a prank.

Leslie then told her friend exactly what had happened. "I was standing across the street from the stadium when I began to feel watched. I thought about crossing to the more brightly lit side when I saw the wolf. It just stood there in the streetlight watching me. I didn't know what to do, so I just froze. That wolf just stood there watching me and I watched it. That's when it did the weird thing. Suddenly, it just stood up on its back legs and it looked just like a person, but with a wolf's head."

It was then that Leslie said she bolted. She ran toward a path and just kept running. She heard noises behind her, but she never looked back to be sure that it was the wolf-thing following. She just ran along the path in a circle. Then she saw Kelly's car and sprinted back toward it.

Kelly didn't say anything else. There was nothing to be said. What Leslie had described was a werewolf! That was just impossible, but one look at her friend's pale face made Kelly a believer.

Red Dog Fox

From the southeastern corner of Pennsylvania comes a whispered legend that has long been part of the fabric of the land around Brandywine Creek. The legend has flowered into a ghostly tale, but before there was the ghost of a man named Gil Trudeau, there was a man whom many claimed was a werewolf.

Gil Trudeau was a rugged young man who was only in his late teens at the time of the American Revolution. Despite his youth, he was a skilled tracker and mountain man. He had a mane of red hair that earned him the nickname "Red."

Gil joined the Continental Army and became a guide for them. In that capacity, he traveled throughout the central states, but it was along the Brandywine Creek, near the boundary of Pennsylvania and Delaware, where he met his fate.

How Gil came to be a werewolf no one seems to know, but by the time he came to the Brandywine, he was already suffering from his affliction. He earned his keep as a guide for the troops, but there were times at night he would slip away. He always returned a day or two later, tired, scratched, and battered, but strangely recharged.

The men he served with began to notice strange things about Gil. He always made his mysterious trips when the moon was full. Some of the soldiers whispered that he must feel the pull of the moon. Others said that Gil traveled then because he could see better in the moonlight.

The men who served with Gil also noticed that they heard strange cries, like the yips of a fox but only more plaintive, during his absences. They claimed that they found mauled, half-eaten animals outside the camp after Gil's return and that he often came back with blood on his clothing.

The men noticed that a strange, foxlike dog followed them when Gil was away. More than once, they saw the large, red fox-beast slipping along the edges of the camp or running through the shadows just beyond the fires. Several men had taken shots at the animal, but it always eluded them. Some of the soldiers remembered old stories told to them at hearth fires long ago. It was said that there were men who sought out or who were infected by strange wolfmen. It was said that these men turned into wolves at certain times, and that they stalked the night hunting like predators.

One night Gil slipped away just as the moon was waxing full. The first night of his absence the men heard the strange doglike cries. It seemed as if the wolves answered the beast's yips and howls. The sounds made the men nervous and they decided to post a guard along the camp to watch against wolf attacks.

On the second night of Gil's absence, a guard walked his path, protecting the sleeping men of the camp. He spotted the large foxlike creature with its reddish fur and quick darting movements. He shot at the beast, but it slipped away as always, like a phantom into the night.

On the third night, the man on watch decided that he was going to kill the beast. It was larger than any fox that he had ever seen before. It was, in fact, larger than a wolf, but it looked more like a fox. The sentry walked his route with his musket loaded, ready to dispatch the beast. The full moon gave the man plenty of light to see by and he kept a careful watch for the animal.

In the middle of the night, the beast slid by in the shadows, but the sentry saw the movement. The man was sitting, leaning against a tree as if asleep, but he had been watching and waiting for his chance. Now he carefully lifted the musket into place and took his shot.

The fox gave a yip of pain and the sentry smiled. He knew that he had hit the beast. The other men were roused by the shot and the animal took off. The men kept a watch for the rest of the night, because the wounded animal posed a potential threat. In the morning, the soldiers decided to follow the blood trail and see if they could find the beast. The sentry wanted the hide and the men wanted to see the massive creature in the light of day. For almost an hour they followed the dried blood. They found it on rocks, on tree branches, and on the exposed roots of a tree where it seemed to have stopped to rest.

The soldiers realized that the fox creature had been making for the waters of the Brandywine Creek. It must have craved water because of the blood loss.

The men rounded a curve in the creek and stopped short. Leaning against a tree at the water's edge was the large red fox. As the men came closer, it raised its head as if to ask for help. It gave a faint whine and dropped its head. As the men stood staring at the beast, it began to change. They watched in horror as the beast seemed to melt or shift shape back into that of Gil Trudeau. The young scout laid there naked and dead. His lovely red hair shifted slightly in the breeze.

The soldiers gave Gil a burial and moved on. They had a war to fight. But at campfires those who had known Gil told his tale over and over again.

It is said that Gil Trudeau's spirit haunts the area where he died. He is seen as both a young man and as an animal. He shifts shape from a fox to a dog to a wolf, and some say he even has appeared as a bear or a deer. But it is as a fox or wolf that Gil Trudeau is most often seen. The local folks call his ghost "Red Dog Fox."

The Dog-Man of Westmoreland County

Matt lived in the town of Delmont and was driving to work one night in 2004 when his life took a sharp turn into the bizarre. On a stretch of two-lane highway on Route 66 near the Green Gate Mall, his headlights picked up what he took to be a person standing along the left side of the highway. Matt slowed down as his headlights picked up the figure. When he was approximately fifty yards away from it, the figure dashed across the road in a strange loping manner that reminded him more of the gait of an animal rather than that of a man. It all happened fast, but Matt was able to see what appeared to be a snout much like a dog's nose, but not as pronounced. He saw no ears or eyes, but he could see that it was not clothed. Perhaps the thing that struck him the most was the physique of the figure. The upper body was massively large, but from the waist down it was thinly framed.

When the creature reached the right side of the road, it dropped to all fours like a large animal and scooted under a chain-link fence that surrounded a power transformer. Matt estimated that the fenced area was approximately thirty square feet. Matt pulled the car over immediately and grabbed a flashlight that was lying on the seat. He flashed the light around the fenced spot, but did not see the creature anymore. He found a dug-out area about two feet deep at the fence, and it was through there that the creature apparently escaped.

Matt eased the car back on the road and continued on his way to work. His strange encounter bothered him enough that he eventually contacted Brian Seech, an investigator from the Center for Unexplained Events. Brian took a report and added to a file he created for such encounters. Matt was relieved to know that he was not the only one to see some strange, anomalous dog-man figure in the area. Brian has had at least one other account within twenty miles of this sighting, and there have been a few other accounts in western Pennsylvania that he has collected.

BIBLIOGRAPHY

BOOKS AND ARTICLES

Arment, Chad. *Boss Snakes: Stories of Sightings of Giant Snakes in North America*. Landisville, PA: Coachwhip Publications, 2008.

———. *Cryptozoology: Science and Speculation*. Landisville, PA: Coachwhip Publications, 2004.

———. *The Historical Bigfoot*. Landisville, PA: Coachwhip Publications, 2006.

Bord, Janet, and Colin Bord. *Alien Animals*. Harrisburg, PA: Stackpole Books, 1981.

———. *The Bigfoot Casebook*. Harrisburg, PA: Stackpole Books, 1982.

———. *Bigfoot Casebook Updated: Sightings and Encounters from 1818 to 2004*. Enumclaw, WA: Pine Winds Press, 2006.

———. *Unexplained Mysteries of the Twentieth Century*. Chicago: Contemporary Books, 1989.

Burke, Michael. "Green Thing Sparks Rumors." *Valley News Dispatch*, March 5, 1981.

Chance, Bob. "Earthline." *The Aegis*, 19 December 1985.

———. *Earthline: A 30-Year Anthology*. Landisville, PA: Coachwhip Publications, 2008.

Coleman, Loren. *Curious Encounters: Phantom Trains, Spooky Spots, and Other Mysterious Wonders*. Boston: Faber and Faber, 1985.

———. *Mysterious America*. Rev. ed. New York: Paraview Press, 2004.

Coleman, Loren, and Jerome Clark. *Cryptozoology A to Z: The Encyclopedia of Loch Monsters, Sasquatch, Chupacabras, and Other Authentic Mysteries of Nature*. New York: Fireside Books, 1999.

Eerie PA Magazine. Issue 1 (Fall 2005) and Issue 2 (Spring 2006).

Godfrey, Linda S. *Hunting the American Werewolf*. Madison, WI: Trail Books, 2006.

Gorden, Joe. "Seeing is Believing." *Johnstown Tribune Democrat*, January 28, 2007.

Green, John. *Sasquatch: The Apes among Us*. North Vancouver, BC: Hancock House, 1978.

Hageman, Dan, and Brian Seech. *Strange Tales of Butler County*. Butler, PA: Self-published, n.d.

Hall, Jamie. *Half Human, Half Animal: Tales of Werewolves and Related Creatures*. Bloomington, IN: First Books, 2003.

Heinselman, Craig. "Three New Pennsylvania Thunderbird Reports." *North American BioFortean Review* 3: no. 2., issue 7 (October 2001).

Hill, Jim. "Bigfoot—Baltimore Trucker Sees Seven-Foot 'Whopper' Near Atomic Plant." *York Daily Record*, 7 March 1987.

———. "Bigfoot—Wild Man of the Woods Roams County." *York Daily Record*, 23 February 1978.

———. "Stalking Bigfoot: Pair Study Sightings." *York Daily Record*, 15 January 1979.

Jarvis, Sharon, ed. *True Tales of the Unknown Beyond Reality*. New York: Bantam Books, 1991.

Johnson, Paul. *The Bigfoot Phenomenon in Pennsylvania*. Self-published, 2007.

Johnson, Paul, and Joan Jeffers. *Pennsylvania Bigfoot*. Self-published, 1986.

Lloyd, Mac. "Huge, Mysterious Tracks Found on Isolated Farm." *The Aegis*, 2 February 1978.

Lyman, Robert R., Sr. *Forbidden Land: Strange Events in the Black Forest, Volume I*. Coudersport, PA: Leader Publishing, n.d.

———. *Amazing Indeed: Strange Events in the Black Forest, Volume II*. Coudersport, PA: Leader Publishing, n.d.

McCloy, James F., and Ray Miller. *The Jersey Devil*. Wallingford, PA: Middle Atlantic Press, 1976.

McGovern, Una, ed. *Chambers Dictionary of the Unexplained*. Edinburgh, UK: Chambers, 2007.

Rodda, Randy. "Bigfoot in County." *York Dispatch*, 21 February 1987.

Seech, Brian. *Bigfoot in Westmoreland County*. Butler, PA: Self-published, n.d.

Wilson, Patty A. *Haunted Pennsylvania*. Laceyville, PA: Belfry Books, 1998.

ONLINE SOURCES

"Are There Mountain Lions in Pennsylvania." *Pennsylvania Mountain Lions*. www.members.tripod.com/~zormsk/mtlions.html.

BURO: Butler Organization for Research of the Unexplained. www.boru-ufo.com.

Center for Unexplained Events. www.center-for-unexplained-events.350.com.

Eppig, Emily. "The Jersey Devil Lives." *Suite 101*. Posted 3 October 2008. http://paranormal.suite101.com/article.cfm/the_jersey_devil_lives.

Gordon, Stan. "Additional Pennsylvania 'Thunderbird' Reports." *Jeff Rense Program*. http://www.rense.com/general14/additionalpenn.htm.

———. *Stan Gordon's UFO Anomalies Zone*. www.stangordonufo.com.

"The Jersey Devil." *American Folklore*. www.americanfolklore.net/jersey-devil.html.

"The Jersey Devil." *DIGESTezine*. www.angelfire.com/zine/digest/devil.html.

Juliano, Dave. "Jersey Devil Story." *Jersey Devil Homepage*. www.the-jersey-devil.com/devilstory.html.

McCrann, Grace-Ellen. "Legend of the New Jersey Devil." *The New Jersey Historical Society*. Posted 26 October 2000. www.jerseyhistory.org/legend_jerseydevil.html.

Pennsylvania Bigfoot Society. www.pabigfootsociety.com.

Pennsylvania Research Organization. www.paresearchers.com.

Swope, Pastor. "Thunderbirds over Western Pennsylvania." *The Paranormal Pastor*. Posted 7 June 2008. www.theparanormalpastor.blogspot.com.

Tiller, Aaron. "Jersey Devil Sightings." *Castle of Spirits*. www.castleofspirits.com/stories03/jersey.html.

Wang, Jessica. "Mountain Lion Killed in PA." *Stanford Daily*. Posted 18 May 2004. www.stanforddaily.com/cgi-bin/?p=1015258.

www.rthomas.clara.net/cb/pa.html

members.tripod.com/~zormsk/mtlions.html

ARCHIVES

Eric Altman, private collection

Center for Unexplained Events collection

Dan Hageman, private collection

Paul Johnson, private collection

Pennsylvania Bigfoot Society collection

Brian Seech, private collection

ACKNOWLEDGMENTS

This book would not have been possible without the help of many people in the cryptozoological community in Pennsylvania. The offerings of support, sharing, knowledge, and help from these people are unprecedented in my experience. I must name them so that they receive at least a little of the immense credit due them.

First, let me thank Brian and Terrie Seech for sharing their knowledge, time, and archives with me. They have amassed a vast library of material on the subject of Bigfoot and UFOs in Pennsylvania. It is an immense undertaking, and they have done so purely for altruistic reasons. They are some of the most giving and loving people that I have ever met. Not only do I owe them a great debt for their invaluable help on the book, but I am lucky enough to call them dear friends.

Through Brian and Terrie I got to meet Dr. Paul Johnson, who has been researching Bigfoot and UFO sightings in Pennsylvania for many years. Paul's work is rarely heard of outside of the small community of investigators in western Pennsylvania, but his documentation and knowledge base is huge. He was kind enough to share some of it with me and to allow me to share it with you.

Eric Altman is the director of the Pennsylvania Bigfoot Society and a dear friend of mine. Eric opened up his own records and allowed me unprecedented access. I have been amazed at the cases that PBS has worked on. Eric's knowledge and patient responses to my questions truly has been a godsend. Eric is a tremendous man and I'm honored to call him a dear friend.

When working with Bigfoot or UFO material in Pennsylvania, the name Stan Gordon comes up continually. That's because Stan has been a consummate researcher for approximately forty years. Stan has appeared on many television shows throughout the years. His greatest fame is as the foremost expert on the Kecksburg Incident, but he's equally knowledgeable about the entire field of Bigfoot and UFO research. Several of the stories in the book were originally researched by Stan. I've never stopped marveling at his immense knowledge. Stan is also a longtime friend, and I've been proud to know him for many years.

There are many others who have influenced my research. I certainly owe a debt of thanks to every person who has had an unusual experience and reported it. I'm sure that it has not always been easy to stand up and talk about the strange things happening in Pennsylvania, but the bravery of those who have reported their encounters has helped to create a vast database in Pennsylvania. Thank you to each and every person who has contacted an investigator and not allowed their story to fade away.

I want to thank Kyle Weaver, my editor at Stackpole Books. Kyle is a writer's dream editor. He's honest, fair, and open-minded. He has embraced my vision for this book and others before it. His constructive comments and guidance have made this book something that I am proud of. Working with Kyle has been a blessing in my life.

Of course, there are family and friends to thank every time. My dear friends Mark and Carol Nesbitt are always an inspiration in my life. Jim Andrews, Craig Rupp, Patty Dulashaw, Charley Helsel, and everyone at GRF always support my work.

Peggy Bookhammer, my mom, is always my cheerleader, and my brother Terry is now and will always be my biggest fan. I'm always so honored by that. Thanks also to my sister and other brothers. I love you all very much.

My most humble thanks goes to my sons, Daniel, Michael, and Ben, who have grown up in what they call "Mom's *X-Files* life." I'm glad that they enjoy seeing the unusual with me. And to Baby Luke, my first grandchild, welcome aboard Grandma's world. He's a joy and my hope for the future. Thanks for coming to love us all, Baby Luke.